BRAVEHEARTS

BRAVEHEARTS

Whistle-Blowing in the Age of Snowden

MARK HERTSGAARD

Hot Books

Hot Books may be purchased in bulk at special discounts for sales promotion, corporate gifts, fund-raising, or educational purposes. Special editions can also be created to specifications. For details, contact the Special Sales Department, Skyhorse Publishing, 307 West 36th Street, 11th Floor, New York, NY 10018 or info@skyhorsepublishing.com.

Hot Books® and Skyhorse Publishing® are registered trademarks of Skyhorse Publishing, Inc.®, a Delaware corporation.

Visit our website at www.hotbookspress.com.

10 9 8 7 6 5 4 3 2 1

Library of Congress Cataloging-in-Publication Data is available on file.

Cover design by Brian Peterson

Print ISBN: 978-1-5107-0337-7
Ebook ISBN: 978-1-5107-0342-1

Printed in the United States of America

Contents

PART ONE

Snowden and His Teachers

B y now, almost everyone knows what Edward Snowden did. He leaked some of the most secret documents in history, revealing that the United States government was spying around the clock on hundreds of millions of people around the world—collecting the phone calls and emails of virtually everyone on earth who uses a cell phone or the Internet—and then lying about it.

Snowden's revelations, published first in the *Guardian* newspaper in June 2013, unleashed a global media frenzy and provoked heated political debate. Outraged privacy and civil liberties advocates charged that the sweeping surveillance, which was conducted without court warrants, violated the Fourth Amendment to the US Constitution and resembled the totalitarian methods of Big Brother in

George Orwell's dystopian novel, *1984*. Equally furious US government officials labeled Snowden a thief and a traitor whose illegal disclosures had grievously harmed the fight against terrorism and compromised Americans' security.

But there is more to Edward Snowden's exploits than this. If you want to know why Snowden did what he did, *the way he did it*, you need to know the stories of two other men.

One of them is Thomas Drake. Like Snowden, Drake worked for the National Security Agency, the vast US government enterprise that was conducting the disputed surveillance. Drake tried to blow the whistle years earlier on the very same practices Snowden later exposed. But unlike Snowden, Drake tried to do it through legal channels. Things did not go well.

Drake held a much higher position in the NSA than Snowden did; as a member of the NSA's "senior executive service," he reported to the agency's number three official. After blowing the whistle—first within the NSA, then to Congress and finally to the press—Drake was arrested at gunpoint, smeared in the news media, threatened with life in prison and ruined professionally and financially. "Hammered" and "crushed" were the words he used in interviews for this book to describe his ordeal. Adding insult to injury, his warnings about the dangers of the NSA's surveillance program were largely ignored by the mainstream media and had very little impact on public awareness or government policy.

But they had a profound impact on Snowden. It was not that Drake inspired Snowden to blow the whistle. Snowden seems to have made that decision on his own, driven by his conviction that Americans in particular had a right to know about the surveillance to which they were subjected and to decide for themselves whether the threats to their liberty and privacy were worth the additional security the surveillance purportedly delivered.

But Snowden did learn vital lessons from Drake about how to turn his ideals into effective action. In particular, he learned how *not* to go about blowing the whistle—in essence, do not go through official channels. And afterwards, he repeatedly credited Drake for leading the way. "It's fair to say that if there hadn't been a Thomas Drake, there couldn't have been an Edward Snowden," Snowden told Al Jazeera in 2015.

And then there is The Third Man. His revelations, never before reported, add a fascinating new chapter to the Snowden story, a chapter punctuated by episode after episode of alleged duplicity, bureaucratic backstabbing and violations of law.

The Third Man was a senior Pentagon official whose extensive—and embattled—involvement in Drake's case shaped Snowden's later decision to commit so-called civil disobedience whistle-blowing (though neither Snowden nor Drake knew The Third Man at the time). While Snowden's leaking of secret NSA documents made him world famous and Drake's misadventures received a smattering of media coverage in the United States, The Third Man has remained in the shadows—until now. In this book, he identifies himself by name and speaks on the record for the first time.

The Third Man has an extraordinary backstory: his grandfather faced down Hitler at gunpoint the first time the future Führer tried to take over Germany, during the 1923 Beer Hall Putsch. The lesson he inherited—"in life, one should always try to do the right thing, despite the risks"—led him, years later, to fight inside the system for fair treatment of Drake, Snowden, and other whistle-blowers. The allegedly illegal, corrupt, sometimes darkly comic behavior he witnessed in response eventually turned The Third Man into a whistle-blower himself.

The Third Man's testimony, if affirmed by judicial proceedings, could end up putting current and former Pentagon officials in jail. (As this book went to press, official investigations were quietly under way.) The testimony also utterly rebuked President Barack Obama's and former Secretary of State Hillary Clinton's shared position on Snowden, putting the lie to their continued claims that Snowden could have raised his concerns through established channels because US whistle-blowing law protected him. The Third Man's testimony suggested instead that the "civil disobedience whistle-blowing" Snowden practiced was the only type that worked for the public interest, though at terrible cost to the whistle-blower.

Tracing the evolution of these three men's overlapping stories reveals much about how whistle-blowing, accountable government, democracy, and public-spirited journalism do and do not work in the United States today. What do we see when the curtain that usually conceals the inner workings of the US government is lifted? Read on and find out.

"What They Fear Is Light"

Like whistle-blowers before and since, Snowden and Drake were harshly criticized for their actions. The condemnations were fiercest from colleagues in the national security apparatus, who disparaged the two whistle-blowers as criminals, naifs, and egomaniacs. More than a few inside-the-Beltway journalists and pundits joined the chorus, asking how any government is supposed to function, much less ensure public safety in a dangerous world, if every federal official is free to substitute his own judgment of what's right and wrong for

that of his superiors. Calling Snowden a "political romantic . . . with the sweet, innocently conspiratorial worldview
of a precocious teenager," columnist Michael Kinsley wrote
in the *New York Times* that decisions about whether to
release government secrets "must ultimately be made by the
government."

But granting the government sole authority over what
secrets can be shared invites other dangers, countered
Ben Wizner of the American Civil Liberties Union, one of
Snowden's US lawyers. "Imagine that since [the September
11 terrorist attacks] the public had had access only to what
the executive branch wanted us to know," Wizner told me.
"We wouldn't have known that the case for war in Iraq was
based on lies and misrepresentations. We wouldn't have
known about Abu Ghraib [the prison in Baghdad where US
forces tortured detainees]. We wouldn't have known that the
US government ran an extraordinary rendition program and
used torture against captured individuals. We wouldn't have
known that the Bush administration disregarded the [Foreign
Intelligence Security Act] and instituted widespread surveillance on American citizens and millions of others around the
world. All of this activity was classified at the very highest
levels and the public only knows about it because there were
brave whistle-blowers who could work with investigative
journalists to bring that information to light. I don't think
anyone could say that American democracy isn't better off
with the public knowing that information."

During my thirty years as an independent journalist and
author, I have recounted the stories of many whistle-blowers
in both the public and the private sectors for such publica-
tions as *Vanity Fair*, *Newsweek*, the *Nation*, the *Los Angeles
Times*, and international outlets like the BBC, *Le Monde
Diplomatique*, and *Die Zeit*. My reporting leads me to argue

that, whether you agree with them or not, whistle-blowers have played a larger role in public life than is commonly recognized, and they deserve our attention and understanding.

And whistle-blowers' role seems likely to grow in the years ahead. At a time when the checks and balances designed to keep American democracy on track have lapsed—when the executive branch no longer bothers to obtain a declaration of war from Congress before launching hostilities; when news outlets have been turned into profit centers that eliminate not only investigative journalism but even basic reporting on public affairs; when Congress seems unwilling to fund government agencies sufficiently to deter dangerous or fraudulent corporate behavior—whistle-blowers offer an essential corrective: they reveal what powerful individuals and institutions want kept secret. This does not give whistle-blowers a blank check to raise unwarranted concerns or carelessly smear reputations. It does mean that their ability to speak out without retaliation should be protected, and when they do speak out, the rest of us should pay attention.

Before Snowden took the fateful step of removing ultra-secret documents from the NSA databases and handing them to independent journalists Glenn Greenwald and Laura Poitras, his biggest worry was that his truth-telling would make no difference. Passing classified information to unauthorized individuals was, he knew, blatantly illegal and invited harsh punishment. Ewen MacAskill, a reporter for the *Guardian* who joined Poitras and Greenwald in questioning Snowden in Hong Kong, asked the young NSA contract employee what he thought would happen to him. Snowden's reply was as bleak as it was concise: "Nothing good." Nevertheless, buoyed by his certitude that he was doing the right thing, Snowden was prepared to give up his highly paid job, separate himself from his family and girl-friend, and perhaps spend the rest of his life in prison.

"I only have one fear in doing all of this," Snowden wrote in his first online conversation with Greenwald: "that peo-ple will see these documents and shrug, that they'll say, 'we assumed this was happening and don't care.' The only thing I'm worried about is that I'll do all this to my life for nothing."

Odd as that may sound in retrospect, it was a reason-able enough apprehension on Snowden's part. The historical record shows that the vast majority of whistle-blowers don't achieve even the collective shrug Snowden feared would greet his disclosures.

Whistle-blowers put their careers, reputations, friend-ships, family ties, physical and mental health, and sometimes their very lives at risk by revealing information powerful interests want kept secret. Then, often, nothing much comes of it. The disclosures attract little or no media coverage and generate no real debate, much less reform, of the policies or behavior in dispute. Meanwhile, the whistle-blower's life fre-quently ends up ruined. The script plays out much the same whether the whistle-blower works for a government, corpo-ration, international organization, religious institution, or other established bureaucracy.

"The only satisfaction whistle-blowers can count on is knowing that they did the right thing," said Thomas Devine, the legal director at GAP, the Government Accountability Project, in Washington, DC, the world's premier whis-tle-blower advocacy organization and another of Snowden's US-based legal representatives.

A stunning case in point involves the US government's use of drones as assassination tools. In October 2015, *The Intercept*—the investigative news site founded by Greenwald, Poitras, and Jeremy Scahill—published a series of reports based on what it called "a cache of secret documents detailing the inner workings of the US military's assassination program in Afghanistan, Yemen and Somalia." The documents were provided by a whistle-blower "who is directly involved with the assassination program," wrote Scahill, the lead journalist on the project. Drone strikes were a central element of the Obama administration's military strategy; proponents said they offered a cheaper, less risky alternative to putting US troops in harm's way, while critics charged that individuals were placed on "kill lists" and executed through secret deliberations, without indictments, trials, or other legal processes. *The Intercept* series "The Drone Papers" contained plenty of newsworthy revelations, including an allegation that many of those killed by drones were civilians (in Afghanistan at one point, an estimated 90 percent of those assassinated were civilians).

Despite these fresh insights into a controversial government program, *The Intercept* series had limited impact, not least because the rest of the media did not treat it as a front-page story. "We received a deluge of coverage in non-mainstream outlets, and a lesser but still significant amount from establishment media," Betsy Reed, *The Intercept*'s editor-in-chief, told me. "The biggest newsrooms, such as at the *Times* . . . noted the leak but did not devote stories to the documents themselves or to our reporting on them. I would hesitate to speculate on the reasons for that omission, but I do believe they would have served their readers well by covering this disclosure, which filled in crucial blanks in public understanding of the Obama administration's signature national security initiative."

Snowden, however, proved to be a sensational exception to the general rule that whistle-blowers get nowhere. Within days, as first the *Guardian* and later the *Washington Post* published articles based on his disclosures, the 29-year-old former NSA contract employee became the most famous—or infamous, if you prefer—whistle-blower in history. His pale, bespectacled, goateed face peered from countless television and computer screens around the world as politicians, pundits, and ordinary people reacted to the news that the US government, beginning after the September 11 attacks, had been intercepting and storing the records of virtually every phone call, email, and website visit made anywhere on earth. Snowden's stated mission—to provoke an informed public debate by revealing secret behavior—was spectacularly validated.

"If you seek to help," he wrote in an open letter accompanying the first documents he released, "join the open source community and fight to keep the spirit of the press alive and the Internet free. I have been to the darkest corners of government, and what they fear is light."

"It Was All Built On Lies"

In terms of notoriety, the only close comparison to Snowden was Daniel Ellsberg, whose release of the Pentagon Papers in 1971 led some to dub him the "grandfather of whistle-blowers." The Pentagon Papers—hundreds of pages of top-secret reports and memoranda that Ellsberg released through the *New York Times* and *Washington Post*—revealed that the US government was fighting the Vietnam War under blatantly false pretenses. Privately, US military and diplomatic officials up and down the chain of command had concluded years earlier that Vietnam was an unwinnable war. Publicly, however, the government issued one claim of impending victory after another, famously invoking "light at the end of the tunnel." Meanwhile, tens of thousands of young men were being sent to fight—and perhaps to lose their lives, limbs, or sanity—in Vietnam while intensified US bombing leveled yet more Vietnamese villages, poisoned the surrounding soil and water, and killed or maimed countless civilians.

The Vietnam War was the most contentious issue in America at the time, and Ellsberg's revelation of the Big Lie underpinning it made him an overnight media sensation. Like Snowden forty-two years later, Ellsberg "outed" himself as the secret leaker in order to shield former colleagues from suspicion. Wearing a coat and tie but starting to grow his hair longer than during his years as a Marine Corps officer, the forty-year-old Ellsberg told a press conference that he was comfortable with the fact that he might spend the rest of his life behind bars. "Wouldn't you go to prison to stop this war?" he asked. Again as with Snowden, government officials, television talking heads, and newspaper editorial pages soon were arguing about whether this self-appointed truth-teller was a hero or a traitor.

Ellsberg's celebrity blossomed further when he unwittingly helped give rise to the Watergate scandal that led to the impeachment and resignation of President Richard Nixon. It sounds like a US history trivia question: why were the burglars who got caught breaking into the Democratic National Committee offices in the Watergate hotel nicknamed "The Plumbers"? Answer: because their previous job for the Nixon White House was to break into Ellsberg's psychiatrist's office, hoping to find damning information about the guy who had leaked the Pentagon Papers. (Plumbers, leaked—get it?)

It wasn't only fame that Snowden and Ellsberg had in common; the two men's trajectories as whistle-blowers paralleled one another in more ways than not. Each, for example, started out a sincere believer in the official American ideology of his day: the Cold War competition with communism in Ellsberg's case, the post-9/11 war against terrorism in Snowden's. "In 2003, when everybody else was protesting [the US invasion of Iraq], I was signing up [for military service] because I could not believe that the government would be lying about weapons of mass destruction," Snowden later recalled.

Both Snowden and Ellsberg also received similarly ferocious criticism not only from top government officials but also from much of the news media and general public. Henry Kissinger, Nixon's national security adviser and a former colleague of Ellsberg's, was heard on Nixon's secret White House taping system calling Ellsberg "the most dangerous man in America," adding that he "had to be stopped at all costs." Nixon told his attorney general, John Mitchell, "We've got to get this son of a bitch. You can't be in a position of ever allowing . . . this kind of wholesale thievery, or otherwise it's going to happen all over the government." Mitchell duly indicted Ellsberg on espionage and conspiracy charges that carried a potential 115 years in prison, but the government's case collapsed into a mistrial when the Plumbers' break-in of Ellsberg's psychiatrist's office came to light.

Four decades later it was déjà vu all over again as Secretary of State John Kerry blasted Snowden as a "coward" who "betrayed his country," adding, "What he's done is expose, for terrorists, a lot of mechanisms which now affect operational security of those terrorists and make it harder for the United States to break up plots, harder to protect our nation." Hillary Clinton was equally harsh during the first Democratic 2016 presidential candidates' debate. Asked whether Snowden should do jail time, Clinton said, "He stole very important information that unfortunately has fallen into a lot of the wrong hands. So I don't think he should be brought home without facing the music."

General Michael Hayden, the director of the NSA during and after 9/11, went so far as to joke about putting Snowden on a government kill list. Hayden ranked among the elite of the elite in the national security state; he was the only person ever to be the director of both the NSA and the CIA, respectively. Appearing at a conference sponsored by the *Washington Post* in October 2013, Hayden noted that Snowden had been nominated for a European human rights award, then added, "I must admit, in my darker moments over the past months, I'd also thought of nominating Mr. Snowden, but it was for a different list." As reported by Brendan Sasso in the *Hill*, "The audience laughed, and Rep. Mike Rogers (R-Michigan), chairman of the House Intelligence Committee who was also on the panel, responded, 'I can help you with that.'"

Former CIA director James Woolsey was even more explicit in his call for Snowden's head. In the wake of the November 13, 2015, Paris terrorist attacks, Woolsey told CNN that "the blood of a lot of these French young people is on his hands," and Woolsey added, "I would give [Snowden] the death sentence, and I would prefer to see him hanged by the neck until he's dead, rather than merely electrocuted."

Which raises a macabre but pertinent question: why hasn't Edward Snowden been captured or killed? Numerous former and current US military officials reportedly have expressed a fervent desire to take out a target they regard as a traitor. "I would love to put a bullet in his head," an unnamed Pentagon official told the website *BuzzFeed* in January 2014. It's no secret that Snowden is living in Russia, apparently in or near Moscow. He told the *Nation* in a November 2014 interview that ordinary Russians occasionally recognized him in local computer shops. (They tended to be young and friendly, he added, and surprised: "Snowden?" they asked.) Of course, Moscow is a bustling metropolis of eight million inhabitants.

But it is also a city where the United States presumably has more than the usual number of spies, informants, and undercover operatives. How is it that Snowden remains at large? And how long will that remain true?

Even as they were vilified, Snowden and Ellsberg were also hailed as heroes. Their supporters tended to argue that, yes, they broke the law but they did so for a noble reason: to tell the public things that, in a democracy, the public deserved to know. After all, if the US government considered the Vietnam War a hopeless mission, shouldn't Americans have been told that when being asked to put their sons, brothers, and fathers in harm's way? And if the government believed it needed vastly expanded surveillance authority to keep the nation safe from terrorism after 9/11, shouldn't it have made that argument openly and sought the consent of the governed rather than institute such policies in secret? (Kerry, whose 2004 campaign for president was dogged by accusations of "flip-flopping," again tried to have it both ways, lauding Ellsberg as a "patriot" while blasting Snowden as a "traitor." Ellsberg, who from the beginning praised Snowden's leak as "the most important in American history," rejected Kerry's comments as "despicable" and called Snowden a "hero.")

Snowden tended to receive more support overseas, both from the general public and from political and media elites. When he was stuck in the transit lounge of the Moscow airport after the US government revoked his passport in 2013, he was informally invited to Germany, where many people displayed signs in their windows saying, "I have a bed for Ed." In October 2015, the European Parliament approved a resolution asking the EU's member states to grant asylum to Snowden in view of his "status as a whistleblower and an international human rights defender." But the resolution, which passed 285 to 281, was nonbinding, and since all EU states had extradition treaties with the United States, they would in fact be obligated to send him to the United States if he did enter their territories. The vote nevertheless signaled that many in Europe viewed Snowden as a hero, and it perhaps presaged a deal that would enable him to leave Russia, where his visa was due to expire in 2017. Snowden hailed the European Parliament vote as "a chance to move forward," taking care to assert that it was "not a blow against the US government but an open hand extended by friends."

Both the vituperation and the adulation showered upon Ellsberg and Snowden implicitly underscored the most striking thing the two had in common as whistle-blowers: Each was successful, spectacularly so. Each got his message out through influential news outlets and then saw it amplified when the rest of the media joined in. Each changed the public conversation about one of the most controversial issues of his time. Each triggered substantial policy changes. And while each paid a high personal price—Snowden ended up living in exile, Ellsberg barely avoided prison—the price easily could have been much higher. Agree with them or not, Snowden and Ellsberg indisputably had enormous impacts on the world around them.

In the short term, those impacts were most visible in the sphere of politics, but the greater effects over time were in the realms of mass consciousness and social attitudes.

Ellsberg's immediate motivation for leaking the Pentagon Papers was to help stop the Vietnam War, and many detractors and admirers alike think he did exactly that. Ellsberg, however, does not share these judgments, and not for reasons of false modesty.

Nixon actually welcomed the release of the Pentagon Papers, Ellsberg told me: "He thought they made the Democrats look bad, since they covered the years before

Nixon became president." What worried Nixon, Ellsberg continued, was that Ellsberg possessed other documents that *did* implicate Nixon. (With Ellsberg's permission, Senator Charles Mathias of Maryland, an antiwar Republican, had alerted the White House to this fact.) Ellsberg had only one such document, but it was an explosive one. National Security Council Memorandum 1, which he helped prepare under orders from Kissinger, discussed options for Vietnam, where Nixon was contemplating the use of nuclear weapons. Only because Nixon feared Ellsberg would start releasing dirt on him did he pursue the measures against Ellsberg that helped trigger the Watergate scandal. "If I hadn't copied other documents beyond the Pentagon Papers, and [Nixon] hadn't known that, the war would have continued and he would have stayed in office," Ellsberg told me. "But how many people who are sympathetic to me know that? Not one in a thousand. The story's never really been picked up."

Ellsberg's most lasting effect was to help change how Americans thought about their government. The Pentagon Papers demonstrated in irrefutable black and white that senior US government officials, up to and including the president, routinely lied to the American people and their elected representatives about some of the gravest matters facing the country. Banal as that realization may sound to twenty-first–century ears, it was nothing less than earthshaking in 1971. "Exposing the fact that the government lied was a shattering, revolutionary thing at that time," said Louis Clark, the Government Accountability Project's president. "It was embedded in the culture, this belief that the president and his advisers have the information and the expertise and if only we knew what they knew, we would have made the same decisions. What Daniel revealed is that it was all built on lies."

Living in the Age of Snowden

Snowden's effect on contemporary politics and government was likewise unmistakable but limited. A striking example involves the USA PATRIOT Act, the law rushed through Congress after the 9/11 attacks. The administration of President George W. Bush and Vice President Dick Cheney relied on the Patriot Act to justify the expanded surveillance Snowden later exposed. Until Snowden's disclosures, Congress had voted repeatedly and by wide margins to reauthorize the Patriot Act, dismissing critics' complaints that the law endangered civil liberties. (Not only did the Patriot Act enable expanded surveillance, it canceled habeas corpus rights for the twenty million people in the United States who were not citizens and authorized government agents to search a citizen's house and public library records without notifying him or her.)

In May 2015, mass anger kindled by Snowden's revelations gave rise to a strange bedfellows alliance on Capitol Hill between the liberal left and the Tea Party right that defeated a reauthorization of the USA Patriot Act. Instead, Congress passed the USA Freedom Act, ending the NSA's indiscriminate collection of telephone records and requiring the agency to obtain individual warrants to surveil specific targets. Privacy advocates disagreed about whether the law represented thoroughgoing reform or incremental change, but it marked a shift from Congress's previous rubber-stamping. "Without Snowden's whistle-blowing, Congress would have reauthorized the Patriot Act," said GAP's Devine, who described the new law as "nothing to get excited about but a solid reform that ends the NSA's reality of taking whatever information they wanted and doing whatever they wanted with it."

Snowden's influence on mass consciousness and conduct, on the other hand, was fundamental enough to qualify as epoch-making. In essence, Snowden changed the way people all over the world thought about their cell phones, their computers, their online lives—the defining technologies and behaviors of early twenty-first-century civilization. Thanks to Snowden, people learned they were being tracked by a modern version of Big Brother; their phone calls, emails, web searches, and other online activities were being recorded, collected, and stored for possible future investigation. "You don't have to have done anything wrong," Snowden explained in his first filmed interview with Poitras. "You simply have to eventually fall under suspicion . . . and then they could use this system to go back in time and scrutinize every decision you've ever made, every friend you've ever discussed something with, and attack you on that basis."

Let that last remark sink in for a moment. Its implications are so profound and far-reaching, it may take a while to grasp them. It did for me. I followed Snowden's revelations when they first appeared in June 2013—what journalist didn't?—and I thought I understood the core of his message. But only while researching this book did I comprehend the full truth: *all* of my phone calls, emails and Internet communications during the years since the 9/11 terrorist attacks have been and continue to be collected and stored for potential future examination. The same is true for all of *your* communications.

Should they so desire, NSA officials can retrieve any of your or my electronic communications and learn a great deal about us both. In theory, they now need a judge's warrant to take that second step and would have to take the additional step of requesting the information from private telecommunications companies. But considering how friendly the NSA and those companies have been during the years since 9/11, these safeguards offer cold comfort.

Which is why I took steps while writing this book to install Pretty Good Privacy encryption on my computer, which should make my communications safer from prying eyes. You might consider doing the same.

Like Ellsberg's revelation that the government lied, Snowden's revelations that the government was always watching triggered a shift in how large parts of society perceived and acted on the world around them. Although the knock-on effects can be subtle and hard to trace, history teaches that such shifts can give rise to transformative changes across a range of issues. Learning that one's government has lied about an ongoing war can lead to wondering what else one's leaders may have lied about.

In the 1970s, this train of thought led the US Congress to launch wide-ranging investigations of the NSA and the CIA and impose the first meaningful limits on their activities—the very limits the Bush-Cheney administration would secretly override after the 9/11 terrorist attacks. In Snowden's case, the public and congressional reactions he sparked apparently doomed the NSA's ambition to gain authorization for even more extensive surveillance by passing the Cyber Intelligence Sharing and Protection Act. "Whatever trust was there is now gone," a senior US intelligence official told the *New York Times*. "I mean, who would believe the NSA when it insists it is blocking Chinese [cyber] attacks but not using the same technology to read your email?"

What larger changes Snowden's revelations may unleash will become evident only over time. Critics such as Secretary of State Kerry and former NSA and CIA director Hayden warned that the changes that have already taken place damaged national security. "We're in a different place now, a place called 'less safe,'" Hayden wrote in the *Washington Times* in August 2015. Journalist Greenwald and other supporters countered that Snowden's disclosures were vital to preserving liberty and increasing accountability for government officials who are charged not only with keeping the nation safe but also with upholding the Constitution. "The real issue is not just privacy but the subversion of democracy," Greenwald argued. "[The US government] essentially put the whole Internet under surveillance and never told the American public about it."

What's clear is that none of this would have happened if Edward Snowden had not blown the whistle in the first place. And there's no going back; previously secret knowledge, once dispersed, cannot be "unknown." Like it or not, we all now live in the Age of Snowden.

"No Reason to Destroy a Man"

But we wouldn't be here if not for Thomas Drake. Probably not one in a hundred of the people who know about Edward Snowden also recognize the name Thomas Drake. But Snowden's accomplishments cannot be fully understood without knowing that he was following in Drake's footsteps.

Snowden ultimately pursued a different path than Drake; indeed, Snowden adjusted his strategy specifically to avoid the retaliation that hammered Drake. Had Snowden pursued the same path Drake did—following the rules, blowing the whistle but through official channels—"He would have been taken down immediately," Drake told me. Instead, Snowden followed the model Ellsberg pioneered: leak the documents needed to prove his case to journalists. This entailed breaking the law and all the risks that came with that, but it meant that the disclosures actually reached the general public.

Drake's journey as whistle-blower began near the pinnacle of the US intelligence community on a red-letter date in its history: his first day of work as a full-fledged employee of the NSA was September 11, 2001. Although the agency would soon balloon in size, budget, and reach as the United States responded to the worst attack on the homeland since Pearl Harbor, the NSA already ranked as the world's largest, most lavishly funded spy organization. Created in secret in 1952 via an executive order signed by President Harry Truman, the NSA was the government's code-breaker as well as its all-hearing global "ear": NSA intercepted the communications of foreign governments and individuals and translated this raw intelligence into information usable by the CIA, the FBI, and kindred US government agencies.

Drake, a forty-four-year-old father of five, had worked for the NSA for the previous twelve years but as a private sector contractor. Tall, somber, intense, Drake had been a champion high school chess player whose gift for mathematics, computers, and languages later made him a natural for cryptography and foreign eavesdropping. He worked for Air Force intelligence during the Cold War, including a long stint in Europe monitoring the communications of East Germany's infamous secret police, the Stasi. Now he joined the NSA's senior staff, reporting directly to its third highest-ranking official, Maureen Baginski, chief of the agency's largest department, the Signals Intelligence Directorate, which was responsible for the physical interception of phone calls and other communications.

From this position of honor and accomplishment, Thomas Drake descended into a nightmare that eventually saw him arrested, stripped of his security clearances and government pension, threatened with life in prison, and blackballed from employment in his field of expertise. In the end, he was

reduced to clerking at an Apple store in the Washington sub-
urb of Bethesda, Maryland.

All the while, hovering throughout the stories of
both Drake and Snowden was Michael Hayden, the former NSA boss who was a primary target of both men's
whistle-blowing.

Michael Hayden was, as previously noted, unique in the
history of the American national security elite: he is the
only person to have directed both the NSA and the CIA.
The former four-star Air Force general served under both
Democrats and Republicans; Bill Clinton nominated him to
run the NSA in 1999, a job he held until 2005, and George
W. Bush nominated him to head the CIA, a post he occupied
from 2006 until 2009. At age seventy, when he was interviewed for this book, Hayden still had the take-charge atti-
tude and solid build of the quarterback he was in Catholic
grade school, though his head was bald now except for a lau-
rel of close-cropped silver hair.

Hayden grew up working class Irish in Pittsburgh—his
father was a welder—and in Washington his ability to convey
complex issues in language an ordinary person could understand made him the briefer of choice when presidents, members of Congress, or journalists needed to be told what he and
his colleagues were up to in the shadowy worlds of electronic
eavesdropping and covert operations. Thus Hayden was the
chief public spokesman for the Bush administration after the
New York Times in December 2005 published the first exposé
describing some of the expanded post-9/11 surveillance programs. Hayden also took the lead in publicly defending the
administration's use of waterboarding and other forms of torture—or, as he preferred to label them, "high-end interrogation techniques"—against suspected terrorists. "I lean pretty
far forward in trying to explain what American espionage

does for the American democracy," Hayden told me. "And I'm quite happy to do it."

Hayden believed that the US government would have been better off if it had been even more open with the news media and the public *before* Snowden made his disclosures.

"When I was at NSA," Hayden recalled, "I used to draw three Venn ovals—one labeled 'feasible,' one labeled 'effective,' the third labeled 'legal'—and where those three [overlapped], that was the space that espionage and NSA in particular worked in. By the time I got to the CIA [in 2006], I realized there was a fourth Venn oval I was missing: politically sustainable. For something to be done over a long period of time required political sustainability. . . . And frankly, you don't get political sustainability without—fill in the blank here—public acceptance, public support, public tolerance. You need that.

"My first summer at the CIA," Hayden added, "we convinced the president to go public with the detentions and interrogations program. We pushed a lot of information out the door on the grounds that this [program] was not sustainable over the long term without some measure of political support, political support would not be forthcoming without public support, and public support wouldn't be forthcoming without giving more information to the American public."

Political adversaries spoke of Hayden with a mixture of respect and loathing. "I'm pretty sure Michael Hayden is a vampire," Ben Wizner, director of the Speech, Privacy and Technology project at the American Civil Liberties Union and another one of Snowden's US-based attorneys, said with a nervous chuckle. A devoted Catholic throughout his life, Hayden made a point in our interview of mentioning his weekly attendance at Mass. When Congress was considering his nomination to head the CIA, he testified that as a youth he benefited from eighteen years of Catholic education. Ray McGovern, a retired twenty-seven-year veteran of the CIA and also a committed Catholic, found Hayden's professions of faith hard to square with the general's defense of torture. "I only had seventeen years of Catholic education," McGovern told me, "so I guess I missed the course on 'Ethical High-End Interrogation Techniques.'"

Hayden took a lifelong military man's view of whistle-blowing. Orders were orders, not options. As long as they were lawful orders—and government lawyers had found both warrantless surveillance and "high-end interrogation" to be lawful, Hayden argued—no underling had the right to ignore or circumvent them. Anyone who did, he told me, should face justice that was "swift and certain."

When asked what role whistle-blowers should play as the nation struggled with the tension between liberty and security, Hayden made no mention of any possible benefits of whistle-blowing. His only expressed concern was to prevent future instances of "unauthorized disclosure" of privileged information. It was a mistake, he said, to pursue punishment through the courts, a process that was "slow moving, with doubtful results and has available to it only very powerful statutes." It was better to handle such matters administratively, he added: "Stripping a person of a clearance, if that's done quickly and effectively, would have a powerful deterrent effect, rather than a small number of showcase trials based on legislation almost a century old." [Hayden was referring here to the Espionage Act of 1917, which was used to prosecute Drake, among others.]

Thus Hayden distanced himself from the government's campaign of judicial harassment and prosecution of Drake. "I had nothing to do with [the prosecution of Drake]," Hayden told me. If it were up to him, Hayden added, "I would have ripped his clearance away, kissed him on both cheeks and sent him on his way. No reason to destroy a man."

Or was there?

Could the NSA Have Prevented the 9/11 Attacks?

Drake's most explosive allegation—one not fully ventilated until now—directly implicates Hayden in what would rank among the worst blunders in the history of spycraft: under Hayden's leadership, Drake told me, the NSA was "culpable for 9/11. The NSA had information that could have stopped the 9/11 terrorist attacks, and it failed to act on it."

Months before the attacks, according to Drake, the NSA came into possession of a phone number in San Diego that was being used by two of the hijackers who subsequently crashed planes into the World Trade Center. The agency did not act on this information, however, and likely was not even aware it possessed it. Adding insult to injury, said Drake, Hayden— egged on by Bush and Cheney after the attacks to "do more" to protect the homeland—then used the catastrophe of 9/11 to justify an illegal expansion of NSA's surveillance efforts to include not just foreign but also US communications. The new authority was needed, Hayden argued, if the nation was to thwart future terrorist threats.

"Hayden has been the main espouser of the Big Lie that we could have stopped 9/11 if we'd have had the mass surveillance that he put in place after the attacks," Drake told me in July 2015. "That is a lie, and Hayden knows it's a lie."

Hayden dismissed Drake's accusation as conspiratorial nonsense, asking me, "If that were true, why wouldn't the presidential commission [that was impaneled to investigate US intelligence failures regarding 9/11] have found that out about us? And by the way, why wouldn't we admit it? We came 'Full Monty' on [having overlooked] those two interceptions [of al-Qaeda chatter] on September 10th, the ones about 'The match begins tomorrow' and 'Tomorrow is Zero Hour.'"

Drake is hardly the first person to accuse the US intelligence apparatus of dropping the ball in advance of September 11. Nor is the NSA the only alleged culprit; the FBI and the CIA have also been the object of withering critiques.

One of the most publicized came from another whistle-blower: Coleen Rowley, the FBI agent later named one of *Time*'s Persons of the Year in 2002. Rowley was working in the Minneapolis office of the FBI when she began developing information on Zacarias Moussaoui, a Saudi immigrant who worked for Osama bin Laden and later became known as "the 20th hijacker."

Moussaoui attracted the local FBI's notice partly because of his interest in learning how to pilot a 747 at a flying school in Minnesota. Six months before 9/11, Rowley and her colleagues in Minneapolis repeatedly requested a warrant to search Moussaoui's belongings, but FBI headquarters in Washington denied the requests. In frustration, Rowley and her colleagues finally passed their information to the CIA's counterterrorism unit—only to be chastised by FBI headquarters for breaching protocol. Moussaoui was duly arrested in August 2001, weeks before the 9/11 attacks; when interrogated, he said that anyone who killed civilians who had harmed Muslims would be a "martyr."

Somehow, this information never sparked the FBI to take further steps that might have uncovered the other nineteen hijackers' plans. Indeed, FBI director Robert Mueller insisted for months after 9/11 that the FBI had possessed no such information on Moussaoui—until Rowley sent a corrective letter to him and the Senate Intelligence Committee.

By then, Congress, the media and the American people had been seeking answers for months: what had gone wrong at the NSA, the CIA, the FBI, and other US government agencies to allow Osama bin Laden's operatives to avoid detection before September 11? At the NSA, Drake was tasked with preparing the agency's response to Congress, a mission that required an in-depth investigation of NSA's practices prior to 9/11.

As Drake interviewed NSA colleagues and scoured databases and records, he came across information that horrified him. It appeared that, mere weeks after the 9/11 attacks, the NSA had secretly revised its scope of operations. The NSA had long been authorized to act solely against foreign entities; eavesdropping on domestic communications was strictly forbidden. Drake had no qualms about lawful surveillance of potential terrorists—far from it. But his investigations persuaded him that the NSA was now turning its vast surveillance powers inward as well as outward, collecting information on communications *within* the United States. And it was doing so without obtaining legally required court orders in advance.

Drake's objections were practical as well as legal. He was not a lawyer, but such domestic surveillance seemed to violate the statutes prohibiting NSA operations within the United States, and doubly so when it was conducted without a warrant; the Fourth Amendment prohibited the government from searching a person's house, papers, or personal effects without a warrant based on probable cause of wrongdoing. Drake also believed that collecting the huge amounts of additional information the expanded surveillance generated could actually *hinder* effectiveness: it created so many additional haystacks that NSA analysts would find it harder to recognize the truly important needles they contained.

An additional shocking discovery convinced Drake that too many haystacks of data had been a problem even *before* the 9/11 attacks. It was well known that bin Laden had ordered the attacks from his cave in Afghanistan, but the operational logistics were largely coordinated from an al-Qaeda "safe house" in the Arabian Peninsula state of Yemen. By early 2001, this safe house was well known to the NSA and the CIA; after all, bin Laden's forces had already carried out a series of other attacks on US targets, including bombing the USS *Cole* warship in 1998 and a failed attempt to destroy the Twin Towers in 1993.

The NSA had already put in place so-called cast-iron coverage on the al-Qaeda safe house, James Bamford reported in *Foreign Policy* in August 2015—the first exposé of this aspect of NSA's alleged pre-9/11 failure. Bamford, a former NSA officer, was widely regarded, on the basis of his four previous books and countless articles, as the world's leading outside expert on the NSA. His article explained that "cast-iron" meant that the NSA intercepted every phone, email, and other form of communication that went in or out of the safe house. Among those communications were at least seven phone calls from an apartment in San Diego where two of the 9/11 hijackers, Khalid al-Mihdhar and Nawaf al-Hazmi, resided for months before the attack.

What Drake discovered, he told Bamford, was that the NSA had intercepted those seven phone calls from San Diego, stored the phone number in its records months before 9/11, but inexplicably taken no further action. Drake found a record of the intercepted calls buried in an NSA database. Since both the NSA and CIA recognized the supreme importance of the al-Qaeda safe house, why would seven phone calls to that safe house from the same number in San Diego not trigger further action on NSA's part? Surely a judge would have issued a warrant so the FBI could surveil the San Diego apartment. Such surveillance likely would have uncovered the plans of the two hijackers and perhaps those of their fellow conspirators as well.

"With 9/11, [Hayden] presided over possibly the single greatest failure of the NSA ever," Drake told me. "He was in charge. He was the captain of the ship. It was on his watch that NSA failed in providing the common defense of the country."

Hayden emphatically rejected these accusations. His voice rising to a shout, he denounced Bamford as someone who wrote "often about the NSA—often, not well," adding that his accusation about the NSA's surveillance of the Yemeni safe house "wouldn't violate the laws of the United States, it would violate the laws of physics!"

"They're Just Buffaloing Everyone"

Later in our interview, Hayden seemed to regret losing his cool, telling me, "Despite, you know, my raising my voice more than once, my instincts are not to bear these people any ill will." But Hayden did not back off his insistence that the scenario in Bamford's article was literally a physical impossibility. "Nothing in the physics of the intercept or the contents of the call, even in retrospect," he told me, "would allow us to determine that one end of the call was in San Diego, or anywhere in the United States."

Hayden also genially disparaged statements to the contrary by Michael Scheuer, the former head of the bin Laden desk at the CIA. Bamford had quoted Scheuer complaining that the CIA had asked NSA some 250 times for information it was collecting from surveillance of the Yemeni safe house but never got so much as a reply. "Mike Scheurer is a wonderful guy, I sometimes see him at Mass on Saturdays, Mike and I chat," Hayden told me. But, he added, "Mike doesn't know the physics."

Hayden then explained "the physics" to me, saying of his former agency, "We never collect the uplink. We always collect the downlink. That's why when you do Satcom [satellite communications] intercepts, you need antennas all around the globe in the footprint of all the possible downlinks; thereby if you can collect both downlinks, to either end of the conversation, you actually then can have computers that connect those two ends of the conversation and give you the totality of the back and forth: he said, she said." But, Hayden repeated, "We don't collect the uplinks."

Who's telling the truth here, one might wonder, and what exactly are uplinks and downlinks?

The latter question is straightforward enough. In the case of calls between San Diego and Yemen, the "uplink" would refer to calls made from San Diego to Yemen—because the call traveled "up" from San Diego to a satellite—and the "downlink" would refer to calls received in Yemen, because those calls traveled "down" from the same satellite. Hayden seems to have been telling me that the NSA, in accordance with the legal prohibition against eavesdropping inside the United States, did not intercept calls originating in the United States—"uplinks." And since it only intercepted downlinks, the NSA couldn't possibly know where those calls to Yemen originated.

As I explored this argument after our interview, I discovered that Hayden had made the same point numerous times before, including in his testimony to the Armed Services Committee in 2006, when the US Senate was considering his nomination to become CIA director. And a number of high-ranking officials had been persuaded by it, apparently including President Barack Obama. In 2014, when Obama explained his decision to back continuation of NSA's domestic surveillance (though with limited reforms), he said, "One of the 9/11 hijackers, Khalid al-Mihdhar, made a phone call from San Diego to a known al-Qaeda safehouse in Yemen. The NSA saw that call but it could not see the call was coming from an individual already in the United States."

But when I checked Hayden's assertions with technical experts, only one of them gave it any credence, and that required giving every possible benefit of the doubt to Hayden's veracity. "The NSA doesn't lie, per se, as much as we might think," said Lee Tien, a senior staff attorney at the Electronic Frontier Foundation, a nonprofit group devoted to "defending your rights in the digital world" whose board of directors includes both Snowden and Ellsberg. "Rather, they use words creatively in a Humpty Dumpty sort of way, without explaining how their words don't mean what we think [they do]."

When I asked Bamford to comment, he described as "very odd" Hayden's claim that Bamford wrote "often but not well" about the NSA. He noted that his books and articles had led to invitations for him to "testify under oath as an expert witness on intelligence issues before committees of the Senate and House of Representatives as well as the European Parliament in Brussels. . . . I've also been a guest lecturer at the Central Intelligence Agency's Senior Intelligence Fellows Program, the Defense Intelligence Agency's Joint Military Intelligence College . . . and Hayden even invited me to give a talk at the National Security Agency's own National Cryptologic School.

"Thus far I've written about NSA missing the calls to San Diego in a bestselling book, an article in *Foreign Policy*, and a documentary for PBS, and not a single person [I interviewed] has agreed with Hayden," Bamford continued. "On technical information, I really trust the people with the PhDs in physics and the senior level career cryptologists that I interviewed over Hayden. . . . He is certainly not a technical expert. And of course he has a very good ulterior motive for his claims: he learned about 9/11 from a $300 office television set tuned to CNN instead of the multi-billion dollar spy agency he was running.

"Hayden not only blew 9/11, he also got it wrong on Iraq," Bamford added. "As I point out in my book *A Pretext for War*, Hayden told the White House that his agency had concluded that Saddam did have [weapons of mass destruction]. That makes him two for two in terms of [intelligence] blunders, the two most serious blunders in modern American history."

Bamford was not a technical expert, but most of the technical experts I consulted held, or previously held, the clearances necessary to understand the NSA surveillance system's internal operations. But no classified knowledge was required to understand how Hayden was misstating the case, I was told, only an understanding of how normal telephone calls work.

Foremost among these experts was William Binney, who spent thirty-six years at the NSA breaking codes and designing surveillance operations before retiring in 2002. A mathematical wizard, Binney has been hailed as one of the most brilliant cryptographers ever to work at the agency. He resigned in 2002 largely because he too was aghast to discover that the NSA had turned its all-hearing ear inwards, directing surveillance operations inside the United States.

Like Drake, Binney tried to blow the whistle on these practices and paid a price. Also like Drake, Binney played an unwitting role in Snowden's leak of documents proving the point. (When Greenwald, the first journalist Snowden approached, did not respond to repeated queries, Snowden came across *The Program,* a short film by Laura Poitras featuring Binney; the latter described how his NSA bosses had taken surveillance programs he had designed for use against foreign targets and turned them against the American people. "I'm sorry for that," Binney said in the documentary. "I didn't intend that." The film led Snowden to contact Poitras, who invited Greenwald to join her on the story.)

When I interviewed Binney, he acknowledged that he was not neutral about Hayden's policies as NSA director. But he said that these policy differences were irrelevant to Hayden's technical description of how satellite intercepts work, which Binney regarded as misleading—or perhaps merely ignorant—gobbledygook.

"He doesn't understand what he's saying," Binney said. "He may be confused about how the system worked, so when he tried to relay it to you, he tried to bluff his way through. That's what the intelligence community has been doing with Congress and everybody else—acting like it's so complicated that they can't understand it. And it's not. It takes a bit of thinking, but it's not that difficult to work out. They're just buffaloing everyone and nobody is taking the time to think it through or question it in any detail."

Forget all of Hayden's talk about uplinks and downlinks, Binney said; that's either an intentional distraction or evidence of how poorly he understood the technical workings of satellite surveillance. Even if you take Hayden's statement—"We never collect the uplink"— at face value, Binney said, the NSA's intercept of the downlink would still have revealed the phone numbers of the San Diego hijackers.

"It doesn't matter which you're collecting, the uplink or the downlink," Binney told me. "The same information travels along either side [of any phone call]. It has to, or the call can't connect. If I call you, I type in the routing—your phone number—that's needed to get my call through the telephone system's switches to your phone. That routing automatically carries my number to your number so your number can be connected back to me. Otherwise we couldn't talk to one another. That's how caller ID works: my number automatically goes with the call, and you can see it on your end before you pick up." (This is how all telephone calls work, Binney added, whether they are made between cell phones or landlines, crossing oceans or connecting neighbors in adjoining apartments.)

But why would Hayden misstate something so easily checked, I asked. Why would a man who cares as much as Hayden does about his relationship with the media endanger it by insisting on a story that doesn't hold water?

"I'm guessing that he's assuming that there are numbers only on one end of the communication—that if you look at the uplink from the Yemeni safe house to the satellite, that it will only show the number in Yemen," Binney replied. "Hayden doesn't know the physics either."

I went back to General Hayden to request clarification of his remarks. I noted that none of the technical experts I'd consulted had confirmed his description of how satellite intercepts of phone calls worked. I asked if he could rebut their objections or put me in touch with an expert who could.

Hayden's full response on this point follows (apologies in advance for his opaque first two sentences; he appears to have replied in haste): "The uplink reference is not connected [to the safe house controversy]. That's a FORNSAT [foreign satellite] issue. That said, I repeat . . . nothing in the physics of the intercept or the content of the calls told us that the callers were in [San Diego]. NSA has consistently testified to that effect . . . not just me. Keep in mind that we are *not* the phone company. We collect as best we can from *outside* the system."

Playing By the Rules

Putting aside whether Drake or Hayden is right about the NSA having missed 9/11, the key question as far as Drake's whistle-blowing is, what did he do with the information he uncovered?

In a phrase, Drake obeyed the rules. As a career military man, he followed established procedures and went up the chain of command to inform his superiors of what he regarded as questionable conduct. He first shared his concerns with a small number of high-ranking NSA officials and then with the appropriate members of Congress and staff at the intelligence oversight committees of the US Senate and House of Representatives.

A straight arrow since high school—he once gave the police the names of classmates he suspected of selling pot—Drake continued as an adult to take matters of right and wrong very seriously. "I took an oath to uphold and defend the Constitution against all enemies foreign and domestic," he told me. "I also had an obligation as an intelligence officer to report instances of 'waste, fraud and abuse.' This was clearly such an instance."

In Drake's mind, the President's Surveillance Program, as it was known, recalled the totalitarian mindset of the East German Stasi secret police on whose communications he had eavesdropped during the Cold War. "You don't spend year after year listening to a police state without being affected, you just don't," he told me. "I remember saying to myself at the time, *Wow, I don't want this to happen in our country!* How could you live in a society where you always have to be looking over your shoulders, not knowing who you could trust, even in your own family?"

Drake could outline his concerns only to a handful of colleagues at NSA because the surveillance programs at issue were some of the most secret in government; very few individuals had the security clearances required to discuss them. The same constraint pertained on Capitol Hill. When he appeared before the Joint Inquiry into Intelligence Community Activities before and after the Terrorist Attacks of September 11, 2001, Drake provided voluminous written and oral testimony but delivered it in "closed" sessions that only members of Congress and staff who held the necessary top-level clearances could access.

Drake spent countless hours in these sessions but eventually came to the conclusion that no one in a position of authority wanted to hear what he was saying. Or at least they didn't want to do anything about it. When he told his boss, Ms. Baginski, that the NSA's expanded surveillance following 9/11 seemed legally dubious, she reportedly told him to drop the issue: the White House had ruled otherwise.

The reaction of Congress was even more suspicious, said Drake. "All the information I gave to congressional investigators seems to have disappeared," he told me. "The only thing left on the record is the fact that I testified. One congressional staffer told me that what I'd told the inquiry was considered so secret that the NSA wouldn't even let it be included in the highly classified version of the final report."

As more time passed and no action was taken—except that the President's Surveillance Program expanded—Drake decided he had to do more. If playing by the rules did not compel his colleagues in the executive and legislative branches to act, he would take his concerns to the press; perhaps public exposure would trigger reform. In November 2005 Drake anonymously contacted a reporter, Siobahn Gorman, at the *Baltimore Sun*, the hometown paper for the NSA, whose headquarters were in Fort Meade, Maryland.

In his dealings with the reporter, Drake said, he continued to obey government security rules: he never divulged classified information; he only described in general terms what he saw going on inside the NSA and advised how to independently confirm his claims.

The resulting articles began appearing in the *Baltimore Sun* in May 2006. Perhaps because the newspaper was not perceived as a major player within official Washington, the articles created little stir outside of the intelligence community. Within the community, however, the response was volcanic. Vice President Cheney himself reportedly ordered that the leaker be found and punished.

"I figured I would lose my job" if discovered as the leaker behind the *Baltimore Sun* articles, Drake said, "but I could live with that. This was about something much bigger than me. I served in the military, and you knew that if you had to, you would put your life on the line for the greater cause of liberty and freedom."

Drake ended up losing much more than his job. On November 10, 2007, federal agents with guns drawn raided his house in suburban Maryland. He was indicted under the Espionage Act on ten counts that carried a potential penalty of thirty-five years in prison—in effect, the rest of his life. He was publicly vilified: most daily media coverage emphasized the Bush administration's characterization of him as an alleged criminal who had compromised some of the nation's most valuable defenses against terrorism. Drake's security clearances were rescinded, rendering him effectively unemployable (such clearances are a prerequisite for most security work, including in the private sector). Former colleagues were ordered not to have further contact with him; any who did would face similar punishment.

As detailed below, Drake fought back against the government's efforts to imprison him and eventually prevailed. Jesselyn Radack, another GAP attorney, was instrumental in his defense, helping arrange a feature article in the *New Yorker* that provided a contextual portrait of his actions. A brief appearance on the TV news show *60 Minutes* further enhanced his public profile. These spasms of publicity did not, however, propel Drake's revelations into the kind of continuing news story that commands the attention of the rest of the media or the political class in Washington, much less the general public. Had Edward Snowden not come along, the NSA's warrantless surveillance program therefore might never have been fully exposed.

In retrospect, the whistle-blowing experiences of Drake and Snowden were different in two key respects. Unlike Snowden, Drake had little impact on public awareness. And Drake's whistle-blowing brought him to the edge of financial and personal ruin. He nearly lost his house. He sacrificed an estimated one million dollars in lost income and legal fees, plus nearly as much in foregone retirement payments. He and his wife separated (but later reconciled) and he lost countless professional friendships.

Nevertheless, Drake said that the government never broke him psychologically, perhaps in part because of the inner strength he had developed as a child. He did not volunteer the insight, but when I asked, he confirmed that part of his emotional resilience, and his sense of justice, stemmed from growing up as the son of a violent father.

"My dad used to beat me up," Drake acknowledged. "But he could never get to the essence of me, no matter how badly I was abused. I had to hide myself at times in gym class. The worst part of it was in fifth, sixth and seventh grades; I would never take my clothes off in front of other kids because it would beg too many questions. The belt was his favorite. . . . What I did have was my mind and my spirit. As I read more and more history and pondered it, I saw that it wasn't just me who was treated unjustly. And I had to ask, 'Why do we treat each other this way?'"

Notwithstanding the price he paid for blowing the whistle, Drake said he would do it all again if necessary. "No, I don't regret it," he told me. "There are things I would do differently, but I don't regret it. The government has incredible powers at its disposal, and when it abuses those powers, someone has to stand up."

Civil Disobedience Whistle-blowing Is What Works

Edward Snowden was already contemplating going public when he, like everyone else at the NSA, began following Drake's case. Despite being NSA colleagues, they had never met or communicated. After all, the agency employed tens of thousands of people and contracted with private companies for the services of thousands more. Besides, Drake was a much more senior official. But as Snowden considered his options for coming forward, he drew crucial lessons from Drake's experience.

"The case of Thomas Drake represented a turning point in the relationship between the executive branch of government that stands over the intelligence agencies and the actual ordinary Americans who comprise the workers of those agencies," Snowden said in 2015. "From day one when you enter into one of these agencies, it's beaten into you again and again . . . that if you see something that's illegal, that's unconstitutional, waste, fraud and abuse, you have to stand up and say something. You have not just the right but the obligation to try to correct those improper activities.

"Despite that, here we had a guy [Drake] who did absolutely everything right," Snowden continued. "He placed his faith in the system. He saw the warrantless wiretapping of hundreds of millions of Americans. He saw corruption in procurement processes, in standards adoptions, and things like that. He brought it to the IG. He brought it to Congress. And rather than protecting him . . . they actively retaliated against him in the most public, aggressive way, to send a message to everyone in the workforce that things were different now. . . . It doesn't matter whether it looks unconstitutional or unlawful to you, because somebody somewhere said this was ok. And you simply have to accept that. That lesson, that the system was broken, is something everybody at every desk at every agency internalized. We all understood the shift; we could feel the wind changing."

What neither Snowden nor Drake knew at the time was that Drake's whistle-blowing had also provoked a ferocious battle inside the Pentagon agency responsible for handling whistle-blower complaints. This battle is described in Part Three of this book.

On one side stood the individual I've called The Third Man. His real name is John Crane. He was the assistant inspector general of the Department of Defense; as such, his responsibilities included supervising the whistle-blower office at DoD, as well as handling all whistle-blower allegations within the DoD, including from the NSA and other intelligence agencies. Crane was also responsible for communications to Congress and the news media. Unbeknownst to Drake, Snowden, or anyone in the outside world, Crane was urging a fair investigation of Drake's claims as well as protection of his identity.

On the other side were two senior Pentagon officials—Lynne Halbrooks, the Pentagon's acting inspector general, and Henry Shelley Jr., the IG's general counsel. According to Crane, Halbrooks and Shelley ordered Crane to close his investigation of Drake's accusations and to identify Drake to the Bush administration officials hunting for the leaker(s) behind the *New York Times* December 2005 article about the NSA's expanded surveillance.

Henry Shelley declined to be interviewed for this book. In an email, he told me, "Most of the topics you indicated you wanted to discuss would necessitate me discussing information covered by attorney client privilege and/or various federal laws protecting the privacy of individuals. I am confident when this matter is fully resolved no wrongdoing on my behalf will be identified." He added, "I trust you will be fair to all involved."

I replied that I strive to "be fair to all involved" in everything I write but that this can be difficult when one lacks a full accounting of the facts. I appealed to Shelley's boss, Glenn Fine, the Defense Department's inspector general, in January 2016 and, in this context, Shelley's client. I asked Fine to "free Mr. Shelley from these constraints" and allow him "to speak on the record about the allegations against him and the DoD OIG." Responding through a spokeswoman, Fine declined my request without offering an explanation.

Lynne Halbrooks did not respond to my repeated requests for an interview.

Like Drake, John Crane thought government officials should play it straight, regardless of how politically troubling a given revelation might be. "I tried to make sure there would never be an Edward Snowden," Crane told me. "Since I was in charge of the [Department of Defense's] whistleblower hotline, I set up both a secret and a top secret channel where intelligence employees, both civilians and military, could forward disclosures to our office without fearing retaliation."

Crane was moved to establish these additional whistle-blower hotlines by the experience of Bradley (later, Chelsea) Manning, a US Army intelligence analyst. In 2010, Manning leaked thousands of classified or sensitive government documents to WikiLeaks, a nonprofit organization that specialized in publishing secret information provided by anonymous sources. Manning's most attention-grabbing disclosure was video shot by US attack helicopters in Iraq that showed in real time the slaughter of noncombatants, including two journalists for Reuters and two children. "Look at those dead bastards," one US airman exults on the video. Another smirks, "Well, it's their fault for bringing their kids into a battle."

Manning gave the documents to WikiLeaks without knowing much about the organization, its anti-establishment politics or its open-source style of publishing. WikiLeaks shared some of Manning's documents with the *Guardian*; together, WikiLeaks and the *Guardian* then invited the *New York Times, Der Spiegel* magazine in Germany, *Le Monde* newspaper in France, and *El Pais* newspaper in Spain to join in a consortium to publish a selection of the most newsworthy revelations, though only after these traditional news organizations' journalists had vetted these revelations and put them into context. Other documents WikiLeaks simply posted in bulk on the web, letting the chips fall where they may.

Unlike Snowden later, Manning did not have much of a strategy for making his disclosures. He was simply appalled by the violence and corruption he was learning about as part of his job. "I just couldn't let these things stay inside my head," he later explained. His one guiding principle seems to have been a belief that the American public had a right to know how its tax dollars and national honor were being deployed in Iraq. "I want people to see the truth regardless of who they are, because without information, you cannot make informed decisions as a public," he said. "I feel, for some bizarre reason, it might actually change something. Or maybe I'm just young, naive and stupid."

Certainly it was foolish of Manning to confide what he had done to a stranger he met online, a stranger who then informed US authorities. Manning was duly arrested and charged with violating the Espionage Act. After being taken into custody, Manning announced that he had felt female from a young age and henceforth wanted to be called Chelsea, not Bradley. In July 2013, roughly a month after Snowden made his electrifying disclosures, Chelsea Manning was sentenced to 35 years in prison, which she is serving at the maximum security military facility at Fort Leavenworth, Kansas.

Crane didn't want to see this happen to other whistle-blowers. He was not necessarily against US war strategy, nor did he favor or oppose what Manning had done. He simply was committed to making sure that whistle-blowers could come forward without facing retaliation. Hence his establishment of the secret and top-secret whistle-blower hotlines where "intelligence officials and civilians could confidentially bring forward any concerns without fear of detection or retaliation."

But by then Snowden had long since concluded that trying to raise concerns through official channels was a fool's errand—a guarantee his mission would fail and he would be fired or worse. He explained his reasoning in an interview with the *New York Times* after going public. At the time, furious government officials and inside-the-Beltway media voices were denouncing Snowden for unilaterally deciding that certain types of classified information should be made public. If Snowden had concerns about the legality of the NSA's surveillance programs, the critics argued, he should have conveyed those concerns up the chain of command through the procedures established to handle such matters.

President Obama made this argument shortly after Snowden's disclosures began appearing in the *Guardian* in June 2013. "I signed an executive order well before Mr. Snowden leaked this information that provided whistleblower protection to the intelligence community for the first time," Obama said. "So there were other avenues available for someone whose conscience was stirred and thought that they needed to question government actions."

Hillary Clinton voiced the same objection two years later while running for president. Asked at the Democrats' debate in October 2015 whether Snowden was "a hero or a traitor," Clinton responded that Snowden had deliberately broken the laws of the United States and should face the consequences. "He could have been a whistleblower," Clinton said. "He could have gotten all of the protections of being a whistleblower. He could have raised all the issues that he has raised. And I think there would have been a positive response to that."

But Obama's and Clinton's statements were supported neither by law nor the real-life stories of whistle-blowers such as Thomas Drake. The protections they claimed awaited Snowden were shams in Drake's case, and the "positive response" Clinton envisioned for Snowden was anything but positive in Drake's case. In addition, as a matter of law, Snowden was not protected by federal whistle-blower statutes, because he was an NSA contractor, not an NSA employee.

For his part, Snowden answered his critics by invoking not only the brutal retaliation mounted against Drake but also simple common sense. It was fine in the abstract to urge becoming a whistle-blower, he told the *Times*. The problem in his case, Snowden added, was that his superiors at the NSA were the very people who had put in place the surveillance Snowden was protesting; likewise on Capitol Hill, the Senate and House intelligence committees had already been informed of this expanded surveillance and had endorsed it. "The system does not work," Snowden told the *Times*. "You have to report wrongdoing to those most responsible for it."

A second whistle-blowing lesson Snowden drew from Drake's experience was that taking one's concerns to the media had to be done transparently and with plenty of ammunition. Apparently a canny student of the relationship among the news media, the public, and the government, Snowden understood that a given administration can usually withstand a negative story if that story remains prominent for only a day or three, as the *Baltimore Sun* articles based on Drake's leaks did. What's required to capture the public's attention and put real pressure on a government are revelations that pierce the static of the 24/7 media babble and make news not for just a few days but for weeks on end. That in turn requires not just a single exposé, no matter how sensational, but a continuing stream of newsworthy information.

In this regard and others, Daniel Ellsberg's example from forty years before was at least as instructive as Drake's recent troubles. The Pentagon Papers were published in the *New York Times* over a period of six weeks, with one or more articles appearing each day. As one front-page blockbuster after another was published, a narrative began to take shape in the public mind along with a certain dramatic curiosity: what jaw-dropping revelation would appear in tomorrow's paper, and in the day's after that? The rest of the media soon followed the *Times'* lead, ensuring that the underlying issues were elevated to a prominence that could not be ignored.

A larger lesson of Ellsberg's example was that merely talking to a reporter, especially anonymously as Drake had done, did not suffice: a whistle-blower had to provide official documents that concretely proved his accusations. "If you're going to shoot at the King, you have to shoot to kill," explained Ellsberg. "The media don't want to risk angering the King if they don't have documentary proof." Thus whistle-blowers who leak to the press "have to put out documents, and they have to put out a *lot* of them if they want to have a big effect."

Yet even as Snowden put out a lot of documents, he eschewed the WikiLeaks model of releasing all information at his disposal. He held back certain documents and removed specifics from others, for fear of revealing information that could put US operatives in danger or imperil legitimate security objectives. *Guardian* journalists David Leigh and Luke Harding reported in *WikiLeaks: Inside Julian Assange's War on Secrecy* that Assange had rejected the journalistic convention of not publishing the names of individuals who might be put in danger by such visibility. Assange subsequently denied the charge, portraying it as part of an effort to smear him and WikiLeaks. In the end, the names were not published.

Unlike WikiLeaks, which seemed to revel in embarrassing the US government, Snowden argued that democratic governance did not mean that the public had to know the names of each surveillance target or intelligence operation of the US government. What it meant was that "we as Americans and members of the global community have a right to know the broad outlines of government policies that have a significant impact on our lives." Snowden insisted on giving Poitras, Greenwald MacAskill, and their journalistic colleagues at the *Guardian* and *Washington Post* final authority to decide which parts of the information he disclosed should and should not be published. For all the attacks that partisans of the status quo leveled on Snowden's supposed recklessness, his actions were in fact carefully modulated, which strengthened their impact.

Nothing about Edward Snowden impressed the whistle-blower experts at the Government Accountability Project more than his sheer effectiveness. Yes, Snowden was courageous; yes, his revelations were eye-popping. But during their thirty years at GAP, Tom Devine and Louis Clark had counseled hundreds of whistle-blowers who displayed great courage and brought forward astonishing revelations. What distinguished Snowden was his ability to draw vital lessons from the experiences of previous whistle-blowers and formulate a strategy that avoided the usual bureaucratic traps and delivered extraordinary results. Of course, since releasing classified documents without authorization was unequivocally illegal, Snowden also had to be willing, like Ellsberg before him, to break the law and face the consequences.

"It comes down to the difference between lawful whistle-blowing and civil disobedience whistle-blowing," said Devine. "None of the lawful whistle-blowers who tried to expose the government's warrantless surveillance activities, and Drake was far from the only one who tried, had any success. They came forward and made their charges, but the government just said, 'They're lying, they're paranoid, we're not doing those things.' And the whistle-blowers couldn't prove their case because the government had classified all the evidence. Whereas Snowden took the evidence with him, so when the government issued its usual denials, he could produce document after document showing they were lying. That is civil disobedience whistle-blowing. And in the national security arena, civil disobedience whistle-blowing is what works."

Entering the Tribe

Edward Snowden and Thomas Drake did eventually meet face to face. It happened in Moscow, on October 7, 2013, when Drake joined a small delegation of whistle-blowing advocates who flew to the Russian capital to present Snowden with an award and express their solidarity with him. "It was an extraordinary moment," Drake told me. "It was like meeting myself in the mirror. I had always hoped someone like him would come along after me."

Snowden has not spoken publicly about meeting Drake, and he did not respond to repeated requests, through intermediaries, to be interviewed for this book. But a secondhand account comes from Ray McGovern, the former CIA agent who criticized Michael Hayden's support of torture earlier in this book. McGovern was part of the delegation to Moscow.

"We were picked up in a van and led to what looked like a nice dining room in a restaurant," he told me. "Ed was waiting there for us. I walked in first and said, 'Ray McGovern.' He nodded and said, 'Hi Ray, I'm Ed.' Then Ed's eyes fixed behind me, at Tom Drake. I could tell by his look of wonderment and recognition what Ed was thinking, and I've since verified it with him: *My god, it's Tom Drake. I told the press in Hong Kong that it was Tom's example—four years of the US government threatening to put him in jail—that taught me how to proceed. Here's Tom Drake, who's responsible through his own example for me being successful in achieving my mission. Wow, here he is in the flesh.* There was this kind of awe, recognition, and deep appreciation. I asked Ed a year later, 'Was that what you were thinking?' He said, 'Yeah, man, you got it.' You can tell when something profound is happening, and that was one of those moments."

Whether they knew it or not, the moment Drake and Snowden blew the whistle they entered a tribe. It was the same tribe Daniel Ellsberg had joined in 1971, the same tribe hundreds of lesser-known individuals joined in the years following. A person entered this tribe not via where he or she was born or to whom. Membership depended on a person's moral choices and actions. Did the person refuse to stay silent in the face of apparent wrongdoing? Did the person speak out about that wrongdoing, despite the risks? Did the person then refuse to back down in the face of the retaliation he or she invariably encountered from the individuals or institutions accused? This moral stubbornness despite personal cost is in the metaphysical DNA of every member of the tribe known as whistle-blowers.

"I think it does make sense to think of whistle-blowers as a tribe, because they identify with each other," said Clark of GAP. "Whatever their particular issues or the outcome of their individual cases, they've gone through the same struggles. It's like Vietnam or World War II veterans, there's a camaraderie because of what they experienced that provides that glue in their relationship. When [former GAP attorney] Tom Carpenter and I went to Russia in 1999, it was really interesting to meet with Russian whistle-blowers. We'd brought along some American whistle-blowers, and they got unbelievably attached to one another, even though they had huge differences in culture and language and all sorts of things. It was striking."

Edward Snowden was the only whistle-blower many people of his generation had ever heard of, but in fact he was only the latest in a long line of individuals who had made similar choices and paid a comparable or greater price in their professional and personal lives. If few attained the level of fame and influence Snowden did, some nevertheless made a substantial difference and even managed to live to tell the tale with only limited cost to their careers and emotional equilibriums.

Probably the best-known whistle-blowers are those whose stories Hollywood found dramatic enough to turn into motion pictures. The 1973 movie *Serpico* told the story of Frank Serpico, a New York City cop played by Al Pacino, who blew the whistle on fellow police officers who took bribes, sold drugs, and otherwise made a mockery of their oath to uphold the law. *The Insider*, released in 1999, focused on Jeffrey Wigand, a tobacco company scientist played by Russell Crowe, who revealed that his corporate superiors were deliberately increasing the amount of nicotine in cigarettes to addict customers; Pacino appeared in this movie too as a *60 Minutes* producer who put Wigand's story on the air, despite his own superiors getting cold feet. *Silkwood* (1984) featured Meryl Streep in the title role of Karen Silkwood, a nuclear industry worker who was killed when her car was run off the road the night she was on her way to tell a *New York Times* reporter about unsafe working conditions at her plant.

In Great Britain, one of the most consequential whistle-blowers of recent years, Katharine Gun, was likewise slated to have her story told on the big screen. Gun was working inside the British equivalent to the NSA—the Government Communications Headquarters, or GCHQ—in 2003 when she received an email directing the GCHQ to help the United States spy on other governments' delegations at the United Nations. At the time, President George W. Bush and British Prime Minister Tony Blair were trying to convince the UN Security Council to pass a resolution backing the invasion of Iraq. The email Gun saw was a memo from the NSA telling the GCHQ to collect "the whole gamut of information that could give American policymakers an edge in obtaining results favorable to United States goals." Gun, appalled at how her government was secretly conniving with the United States in the face of public opposition throughout Europe to invading Iraq, leaked the memo to the *Observer* newspaper. The resulting uproar helped derail any Security Council endorsement, leaving Bush and Blair to launch the invasion alone. Gun was fired and threatened with prison but never regretted her actions. She later said: "I've only ever followed my conscience."

In the next tier are whistle-blowers who have received substantial mainstream media coverage, such as the three women *Time* put on its cover as the magazine's 2002 "Persons of the Year": Coleen Rowley, the FBI agent mentioned above; Sherron Watkins, a vice president at Enron Corporation who discovered the irregular accounting procedures that later brought Enron and its customers to grief; and Cynthia Cooper, a vice president at the WorldCom corporation who uncovered $3.8 billion of accounting fraud, at the time the largest such incident in US history.

Scanning the archives of the Government Accountability Project yields another batch of success stories that are less known but no less valuable to the public good. "The history of whistle-blowers really began in the modern era in the United States with Ernie Fitzgerald," said Clark. As a financial analyst for the Air Force, Fitzgerald in 1968 exposed $2.3 billion in cost overruns for the C-5A cargo plane. Fitzgerald made his revelations in testimony to the US Congress, speaking candidly despite pressure from superiors. President Nixon personally ordered that he be fired. "I said get rid of that son of a bitch," the White House taping system recorded Nixon telling presidential aide Charles Colson.

"The point is not that [Fitzgerald] was complaining about the overruns but that he was doing it in public," Nixon later told aide John Ehrlichman. Fitzgerald sued for wrongful termination and was reinstated—fourteen years later. When Fitzgerald finally retired from government service, Republican Senator Charles Grassley of Iowa praised him as "the father of all whistle-blowers" and the inspiration for Grassley making whistle-blower protection his signature issue. Grassley saluted Fitzgerald for proving that "one person [who is] determined to make a difference can in fact make a difference."

Other notable whistle-blowers include Dr. David Graham, a Food and Drug Administration scientist, who sparked the removal of the painkiller Vioxx from the market after linking the drug to 50,000 fatal heart attacks. Rick Piltz, a federal climate policy analyst, revealed that a former oil industry lobbyist whom George W. Bush installed at the White House Council on Environmental Quality was censoring US government reports on climate change. James Hansen, NASA's top climate scientist and the man who put global warming on the public agenda in 1988 when he testified to the US Senate that man-made climate change had begun, likewise spoke out against the Bush-Cheney administration's efforts to gag him. Aldric Saucier, the US Army's chief civilian scientist, helped to defeat additional funding for the "Star Wars" missile defense program after concluding that the nearly $1 trillion dollar scheme was an unworkable boondoggle. As described in more detail in Part Two of this book, whistle-blowers at the Zimmer nuclear power plant in Ohio revealed laughably shoddy building materials and practices, such as substituting junkyard metal for nuclear grade steel and falsifying X-rays on critical safety welds. Their exposés eventually forced cancellation of a plant that was 97 percent complete.

There is, however, no sugarcoating the fact that the majority of whistle-blowers have an experience much closer to Thomas Drake's than to Edward Snowden's, and this is as true of corporate as of government members of the tribe. In his book *The Corporate Whistleblower's Survival Guide,* Devine writes, "For those who think that blowing the whistle is glamorous or a path to recognition, think again. The majority of whistle-blowers suffer in obscurity, frustrated by burned career bridges and vindication they were never able to obtain. The prominent, lionized beacons of hope are rare exceptions, and even most of them pay a horrible price with lifelong scars."

Yet somehow whistle-blowers keep coming forward, a testimony to their, what—moral superiority? Stubbornness? Foolishness?

Clark argues that whistle-blowing is only going to become more frequent and valued in the years ahead because "it's the only way we'll have any chance of dealing with the level of corruption we face in modern society. The federal government seems to have decided it won't provide funding for regulation and media companies are closing their investigative units. Congress passes laws like the Dodd-Frank Act (covering the activities of financial institutions) and the Food Safety Modernization Act, but then appropriates no money to enforce those laws. The task of regulating corporate behavior seems to be falling to whistle-blowers by default."

It's a rare thing in today's Washington, but whistle-blowing is an issue that attracts support from Democrats and Republicans alike, at least in principle. Lawmakers in both parties seem eager to tell the public that whistle-blowers are vital weapons in the battle against waste, fraud, and abuse in both the public and the private sectors. They do not always vote that way, of course; often, loyalty to a certain industry or federal agency trumps a lawmaker's support for whistle-blowing in the abstract. The attacks Republicans and Democrats alike leveled against Edward Snowden—and both parties' silence in the face of the national security bureaucracy's assault on Thomas Drake—are but two examples of a broader trend. "National security whistle-blowing is the last frontier where politicians are unwilling to match their rhetoric with enforceable rights," said Devine.

The most intriguing example of whistle-blowing's potential power is one that has gotten no public attention but could end up transforming American business, costing companies billions of dollars in penalties and sending corporate officers to prison. Thanks to bipartisan support in Congress and decades of behind-the-scenes work by GAP and other advocacy groups, some 80 million private sector workers in the United States now enjoy strong whistle-blower protections, at least on paper. There are even financial incentives for employees to report corrupt corporate behavior. Seeking to crack down on the kind of deceptive insider dealing that fueled the 2008 financial crisis, the Securities and Exchange Commission (SEC) instituted a "Bounty Program" that can reward a whistle-blower who alerts the SEC to corporate wrongdoing. In a stark reversal of long-standing practice, employees can remove incriminating documents from the workplace and give them to the SEC without being subject to legal retaliation.

"The corporations are going crazy," said Clark with a chuckle. "They're calling it a theft of private property and trying to force their employees to sign agreements not to blow the whistle. They even want employees to give any Bounty Program money they receive back to the company."

"There is no question that it is not always easy or lucrative to be a corporate whistleblower," said Jordan Thomas, a partner at Labaton Sucharow, which he describes as the first law firm exclusively devoted to representing SEC whistle-blowers. But Thomas, who as the former assistant director of the SEC helped draft its new whistle-blower policies, insisted that by no means is all gloom and doom.

Passage of the Dodd-Frank Wall Street Reform and Consumer Protection Act created "a different reality" for corporate whistle-blowers, argued Thomas, because it lets them report wrongdoing anonymously. That anonymity means, however, that the public never learns about these whistle-blowers, nor the lavish rewards they can receive. Dodd-Frank stipulates that a whistle-blower who provides information that leads directly to a conviction is entitled to 10 to 30 percent of the total monies recovered. One of Thomas's clients walked away with $35 million, he told me. He added, "There's a public interest to making this [incentive] clear. If we keep telling people that being a whistleblower is going to end badly, people aren't going to step up and report with the frequency we need to prevent another financial crisis."

President Obama has been a strong supporter of corporate whistle-blower rights, but he has baffled advocates by simultaneously being unprecedentedly harsh toward government whistle-blowers. Obama promised as a candidate in 2008 that he would champion whistle-blowers and preside over "the most transparent administration in history." In office, he honored that pledge only in regards to private sector whistle-blowers. Federal employees—in other words, people who worked for him—were a different matter, especially if they worked in the national security sector.

The Obama administration has brought charges against seven whistle-blowers under the Espionage Act, far more than any previous administration has charged. It has also prosecuted, or threatened to prosecute, journalists on an unprecedented scale, while dramatically increasing the amount of government information that is classified. "It's another example of the Obama enigma," said Clark. "Obama has been without question the best president ever on corporate whistle-blowing and the worst ever on national security whistle-blowing."

A full account of American whistle-blowing is beyond the scope of this book, but even the abbreviated version offered here provides an instructive view of the nation's recent history. In particular, the story of whistle-blowers gives a peek behind the curtain of the daily business of government and politics, revealing how the impulses of power and privilege on one hand and democracy and accountability on the other are frequently at odds.

This alternative history has largely been hidden to date, because most whistle-blowers' revelations get little coverage in major media. But the evidence indicates that whistle-blowers have had more impact on American life than commonly realized. When insiders like Snowden and Ellsberg, Coleen Rowley, and Jeffrey Wigand blow the whistle on high-level lying, lawbreaking, or other wrongdoing, the public can benefit enormously. Wars can be ended, deadly products taken off the market, criminals put in prison, scandals exposed.

Of course there can be trade-offs to exposing secrets, as Hayden and other critics of Snowden argued, and not all self-described whistle-blowers are the real thing. During my years of investigating whistle-blowers' claims I have come across some who were driven more by ego or personal animus than by concern for the public interest. Still other would-be whistle-blowers were doubtless sincere but exaggerated the importance of the alleged wrongdoing they had witnessed or lacked convincing evidence it had occurred. So how does one tell the difference between the valid and the counterfeit?

How can rules be devised and enforced to ensure that the channels for legitimate dissent are protected but not overwhelmed by counterfeit claims from moral poseurs?

Will Edward Snowden's example lead to more whistle-blowing in the future or less? What makes a person become a whistle-blower in the first place? Why do a handful of individuals speak out while the vast majority do not? What is the proper balance between a whistle-blower's "freedom to warn" and the government's responsibility to keep the nation safe, or a corporation's obligations to its shareholders? Since whistle-blowers generally rely on news organizations to publicize their concerns and the news organizations benefit in prestige and audience from doing so, what is the proper relationship between whistle-blowers and the media?

Only when Snowden's actions are seen within the context of the many whistle-blowers who preceded him can one understand how truly exceptional his achievements have been. The flip side is true as well: Snowden's example invites us to acquaint ourselves with the larger tribe of whistle-blowers he joined and the tradition of principled dissent they embody.

Part Two of this book explores these questions, seeking to explain why and how whistle-blowers do what they do, the price they pay, and the changes they've wrought. Part Three returns to Snowden, Drake, and Crane, three whistle-blowers whose cases raise profound questions about the future of whistle-blowing—and indeed democratic governance—in the age of Snowden.

Inside the Nerve Center

An Obligation to Make Things Right

His hair was white now. The summer of 1967 was ages ago. But when a friend sent him a photo of his nineteen-year-old self, memories of those adrenalin-soaked days instantly flooded back, and he recounted the story as if it happened yesterday.

The photo showed him from behind: a lanky white kid with hair unfashionably short for the era. A second young man, this one black, knelt beside him. Both clutched sheets of white paper. Facing them, a black mother and father and five children gathered on the porch of a small, plain but sturdy wooden house. Shoeless and wearing the cotton dresses and T-shirts of country folks, the family listened as the young black man made his pitch. The scene looked friendly but serious.

"That's me and my black friend Ralph," said Louis Clark, sitting in a conference room at the offices of the Government Accountability Project in Washington. "We were trying to register black people to vote in Mississippi." Clark had first come to Mississippi three years earlier as part of a missionary trip organized by his church in Illinois. "We went to help build a school for poor kids," he recalled. "The kids were white, but we could feel the racial tension in the air. This was 1964. The church we were building was ten miles outside the town of Philadelphia, where three white civil rights workers were murdered that summer. I went back [in 1967] because I felt an obligation to help make things right."

Helping to make things right entailed risks. Clark's car had out-of-state license plates; many locals didn't appreciate outsiders coming to their state and "stirring up trouble," as they put it. "I got pulled over by cops fourteen times that year," said Clark. "Each time, I thought, *This could be the end.*"

And there was the Ku Klux Klan.

"One night, Ralph and I were meeting with a group of black community leaders, way out in the countryside. Somehow the Klan found out, because as we walked toward our car afterwards, a couple of guys were waiting outside. They started taunting us, pushing, trying to get us to react.

"Suddenly a big sedan pulled up, and that distracted them long enough for Ralph and I to jump into my car and speed off. They piled into the sedan and zoomed after us. We were flying down these country roads as fast as I could drive. I saw their headlights in my rearview mirror, and they were gaining on us. My body flushed with sweat.

"Luckily Ralph was from that area, so he knew the back roads. He had me make a sudden left turn, and the Klan guys went speeding past. They must have turned around pretty quickly, though, because before long their headlights were in my rearview again.

"After what seemed like forever, we saw the local Freedom Center where we were staying, which was a safe zone. I barely slowed down as we spun into the driveway. The Klan guys were so close we could hear them shout rebel yells as their car shot past in the dark. 'Nigger lovers, go home. We'll get you next time,' that kind of stuff.

"I remember I couldn't shut off the car. I literally couldn't turn the ignition key, I was shaking so bad. I was crying, I was scared, I was mad. I called my parents and told them, 'I don't think I believe in nonviolence anymore.'"

Who Coined the Term "Whistle-blower"?

Eleven years later, Louis Clark found himself running a fledgling nonprofit organization called the Government Accountability Project. By then he had completed seminary studies and been ordained as a Methodist minister, regaining his faith in nonviolence along the way. He had graduated from law school and moved to Washington, DC. At a party one night, a friend mentioned an idea some antiwar colleagues had. They were convinced that Daniel Ellsberg was not the only insider who might speak out about wrongdoing inside the military, and they hoped to launch an organization to assist such truth-tellers. Intrigued, Clark offered to work for the organization for free for the first two months, promising with a thirty-year-old's brashness that he would need only two months to prove himself indispensable.

Thirty-seven years later, in 2015, Clark was still there. As president of GAP, he was responsible for setting the organization's strategic direction and soliciting the donations from foundations and individuals that comprise roughly 90 percent of GAP's $3 million a year budget. "Our theory of social change is based on transparency," Clark told me. "Whistle-blowers enable you as a citizen to know what governments and corporations are doing. If it's affecting you badly, you have the means to challenge it. I don't think people are jaundiced about that kind of information. If a hundred people die from eating peanut butter crackers that weren't produced safely, people care about that."

Since its founding in 1978, GAP had counseled more than seven thousand whistle-blowers from both the public and the private sectors, said Clark. The organization helped whistle-blowers defeat some of the most powerful bureaucracies (e.g., the US Department of Defense) and politically connected corporations (e.g., Bechtel) on earth, though it also watched many whistle-blowers endure defeat and punishment. GAP's successes were based partly on shrewd collaboration with the news media; its clients had been featured in virtually all of the major outlets in the United States as well as countless local ones.

GAP also fought on Capitol Hill and elsewhere to add whistle-blower protections to thirty-two separate federal, local, and international laws. Working with Republicans and Democrats alike but championed most consistently by Iowa Senator Charles Grassley, GAP and a handful of allied groups helped to pass the Whistleblower Protection Act of 1989, the Sarbanes-Oxley Act of 2002 (formally known as the Public Company Accounting Reform and Investor Protection Act), the Dodd-Frank Wall Street Reform and Consumer

Protection Act of 2010, and the Whistleblower Protection Enhancement Act of 2012.

If there was such a thing as a nerve center of the whistle-blower tribe, GAP was it. No other group came close to matching the number of whistle-blowers who have passed through GAP's doors over the years, nor the group's record of achievement and influence in so many aspects of whistle-blower law, politics, and practice. Other groups operated in the same "good government" sphere: Common Cause, Taxpayers for Common Sense, and the Project on Government Oversight, as well as Transparency International on the global level. But none of these groups represented individual whistle-blowers, as GAP did. Some private firms litigated on behalf of whistle-blowers, but their clients were chosen based largely on how big a financial settlement might be won. For GAP, public interest was the primary criterion.

"We only get behind a whistleblower who has a public interest disclosure that is relevant to the public on a relatively grand scale," said Beatrice Edwards, GAP's executive director from 2007 to 2015. "We get a lot of people coming to us and saying, 'The guy in the next office is running a small business in the restroom,' or 'My boss comes in on Sunday to use the phone to call his family in India.' We don't get involved in that kind of petty corruption."

GAP emerged from a conference organized in 1977 by leaders at the Institute for Policy Studies (IPS), a left-of-center research organization in Washington. Founded in 1963, IPS had been a central player in the civil rights and antiwar movements, earning a spot on President Nixon's "enemies list." Richard Barnet and Marcus Raskin, the IPS cofounders, had resigned from the Kennedy administration after blanching to hear top Kennedy aide McGeorge Bundy tell a meeting of the Joint Chiefs of Staff, "If this group can't bring about disarmament, no one can."

IPS played a key but unsung role in releasing the Pentagon Papers, according to Ellsberg. Ellsberg had been trying without success to get a senior member of Congress to release the papers by inserting them into the Congressional Record. "About that time I had dinner with Barnet and Raskin and their wives," Ellsberg told me. "They urged me to give the Pentagon Papers to the *New York Times*. Only years later did I find out that they had already tipped off someone at the *Times*."

IPS was also close to Ralph Nader, the consumer advocate whose 1965 book, *Unsafe At Any Speed*, relied on testimony from company engineers to reveal how Chevrolet had chosen an unsafe design for its car, the Corvair. The book was a smash bestseller and made Nader the country's leading public citizen. In January 1971, five months before Ellsberg released the Pentagon Papers, Nader organized a conference to boost the role and impact of truth-telling insiders such as those he cited in *Unsafe At Any Speed*.

Apparently it was Nader, at this Conference on Professional Responsibility, who first coined the term "whistle-blower." In the past, the term carried an odor of betrayal, Nader noted in a speech to the conference: Americans, he said, tended to think of a whistle-blower "as 'a fink' or 'a stool pigeon,' a 'squealer' or 'an informer,' or he 'rats on' his employer." But whistle-blowers deserved the public's respect and thanks, argued Nader, for they were often the first to learn about problems such as unsafely designed vehicles that could endanger the public at large.

The 1977 conference organized by IPS aimed to turn Nader's strategic insight into an operational reality. Ellsberg remained central. "I'm not sure that there would have been a

GAP without Ellsberg," Clark said. "His experiences with IPS were extraordinarily valuable for planting the seed for the creation of GAP. IPS saw the value in someone like Ellsberg exposing the lies upon which that war was founded."

In its early days, GAP was more of a public relations outfit than a legal organization, Clark recalled, precisely because of the problem Nader highlighted—a problem that has plagued the whistle-blower community ever since: is "whistle-blower" really the best name for these individuals? More than a few members of the tribe, then and now, have objected to the term. Snowden said that it "other-izes" people who speak out about alleged wrongdoing when such speaking out should be expected from everyone. Jeffrey Wigand, the Big Tobacco scientist, preferred the term "a person of conscience." In GAP's early years, Clark recalled, "We got heavily involved in trying to change the negative image associated with whistle-blowing. In a lot of our public materials back then you would see red, white and blue flags all over the place."

"Turn Information into Power"

A legal staff began to take shape at GAP with the arrival of Tom Devine in 1978. A precocious student at Antioch Law School, Devine had already coauthored a book describing how President Nixon had secretly tried to replace the government's nonpartisan civil service system with a political hiring system that could reward friends and punish enemies. Devine convinced Clark that GAP should establish a clinic at Antioch that could train students in whistle-blower advocacy and protection and thereby obtain low-cost legal talent. Devine ran the clinic for the next ten years, and it became the chief source of expertise for a group that waged a chronic struggle with financial solvency.

Devine, too, was still at GAP thirty-seven years later. As its legal director, he was the organization's animating spirit, and many were the opponents who had underestimated him. Even in his early sixties, he conveyed a childlike guileless-ness, a mix of flower power optimism and goofy kindness. Short of stature, he was fond of rhyming invented names into questions, as in, "What's the story, Rory?" or "How's it going, Owen?" In a city of almost totalitarian fashion conformity, he donned the lawyer's obligatory suit and tie only when appearing before a judge or a congressional hearing; otherwise, it was jeans, tie-dyed T-shirt, and scuffed Wallabees. In winter, he could be mistaken for a homeless man, trudging along K Street, the pockets of his hooded Army jacket bulging lopsidedly with a mishmash of notebooks, newspapers, a tape recorder, and left-over lunch while over his shoulder he toted a crushingly heavy day-pack with legal briefs he carried home for late-night client calls and writing assignments.

Beneath the disheveled exterior lurked a razor-sharp intelligence and indefatigable work ethic. Devine was an All-American debater in college, graduating *cum laude* and Phi Beta Kappa from Georgetown; he knew how to draft an eighty-page argument for a judge, but also how to boil it down to an eight-second sound bite for a reporter. An anarchist at heart, he loved to battle what he called "the power structure." At GAP, he helped to develop a model of activism that recruited various forms of public support to give whistle-blowers a fighting chance in arenas that, Devine argued, were rigged against them.

"One person against a corporation is not a fair fight," he wrote in his book, *The Corporate Whistleblower's Survival Guide*, adding, "in conventional terms, the deck will be stacked against you no matter how solid your evidence or astute your strategy." To help even the odds, GAP brought the outside world into the fight: "The key to committing the truth and getting away with it is strategic legal campaigns grounded in public solidarity that effectively turn information into power."

Enlisting the public to help whistle-blowers "turn information into power" involved exerting pressure in three mutually reinforcing areas: the legal, where GAP attorneys represented whistle-blowers as lawsuits flew back and forth; the political, where GAP worked to educate and mobilize local people who may be affected by what the whistle-blower exposes; and the media, where news organizations' reporting on whistle-blowers' charges could prove decisive in both educating the public and persuading government and corporate officials to change their tune.

For a group run by lawyers, GAP invested relatively little faith or resources in the legal process *per se*. When Devine said GAP's approach was to mount "strategic legal campaigns," he meant "a holistic advocacy effort that is sort of like a political campaign." The problem with relying on litigation, he added, is that "litigation needs to go to court, which is the turf of the status quo, the whole power structure. The whole principle of the court is that we don't break precedent, we keep doing things the way we always have. Whistle-blowers are people who challenge the status quo. The court's job is to preserve the status quo."

Asked for GAP's theory of social change, Bea Edwards replied, "We see institutions that rhetorically present themselves as working for the public interest that in fact often represent specific special interests. But it takes whistle-blowers inside of those institutions to reveal *how* they favor the special interests. Often these institutions are reliant on public support. If you can show how those institutions are not representing the public, they can lose their public support, and that creates leverage for social change."

"We expose the secrets that the government doesn't want anyone to know about," Devine said. "And we try to make sure that everyone who needs to know about them, from workers on site to citizen groups to politicians to the media, is made aware, too. The whistleblower is the first rock in the avalanche of public revulsion we try to create against the indefensible."

Was it any surprise that Edward Snowden eventually found his way to this organization?

A Backstage Pass

Perhaps here is where the author should declare his personal interest in this story.

I was an unpaid college intern at the Institute for Policy Studies in 1977 when GAP was founded. I didn't attend the conference that gave rise to GAP, but I came to know Clark and Devine as colleagues when I later joined the IPS staff. In 1978 I began working on my first book and didn't spend much time at the office, preferring to write at home. When I did stop by IPS, I sometimes ran into Louie or Tom and heard about their latest exploits. We stayed in touch over the years, and I've occasionally worked with GAP on journalistic projects, publishing whistle-blower-based exposés about nuclear weapons and airline security, the BP oil spill and other scandals in *Vanity Fair,* the *Nation, Newsweek,* and equivalent news outlets around the world.

I therefore cannot claim to be perfectly objective about GAP, or about Clark and Devine. I have long believed, however, that journalistic objectivity is a myth—an apparently noble cover story for journalism that regurgitates conventional wisdom as dispensed by government officials and other representatives of the status quo. As any journalist must know, every step in the journalistic process involves subjective choices, from selecting which subjects get covered and which do not, to deciding which facts and voices are featured in a given story and which are not, how prominently they are featured, and so on. The inevitability of subjectivity, however, is no excuse for inaccurate or unfair reporting; the journalist has a sacred obligation to be not only accurate but fair to all points of view, especially those, I would argue, with which he or she disagrees. Good journalism does not impose the journalist's opinion on others; it provides the information and perspective they need to make up their own minds.

For what it's worth, these guidelines have on occasion led me to disagree with GAP about the newsworthiness of this or that potential scoop. No investigative journalist worth his or her salt simply takes a source's word for it; we re-report the story so we can independently verify what the facts are and try to determine where the truth lies. That process led me to abort one juicy story a GAP client offered when a fair reading of the relevant documents did not substantiate the would-be whistle-blower's allegations about financial malfeasance on the part of a senior government official.

So there you have it. You're now equipped to judge for yourself what kind of guide I am for this book. For my part, I pledge to tell the story as fairly and accurately as I can, without fear or favor, to quote an exemplary journalistic motto that has been honored in rhetoric more than in reality. My long familiarity with GAP may impose limits on my perspective, but I trust it confers benefits as well. After all, from the time of GAP's founding, I've had what amounts to a backstage pass to the de facto nerve center of the whistle-blower tribe, the place where the theory and practice of "committing the truth" has been more vigorously and successfully pursued than anywhere else.

"Just Give Me Ten More Minutes!"

It was nuclear power that first brought GAP and me together in a serious way, because my first book was about the nuclear industry. By 1979, the battle over nuclear power was as hot as any issue in America, and GAP found itself smack in the middle of it.

My book, *Nuclear Inc.: The Men and Money Behind Nuclear Energy*, was based on scores of interviews with top executives at General Electric, Westinghouse, and other leading firms in the industry. I was all of twenty-two years old and I looked even younger, so the executives spoke to me quite freely, perhaps treating me like a friend of their own kids. For example, I asked John West, a nuclear vice president for the reactor manufacturer Combustion Engineering, whether the lack of a solution for storing nuclear waste posed a problem for the industry. West replied that the real trouble was not that there was no solution but that there were too many good solutions and the government, as usual, could not bring itself to select one. "I have a vulgar analogy," the dough-faced executive confided. "It's kind of like you have a blonde, a brunette and a redhead, real glamorous gals all lined up for action, and you can't decide which one you'd like to go to bed with. They're all good."

On the morning the Three Mile Island plant was undergoing the worst nuclear accident in US history, I interviewed a vice president at Westinghouse. At the time, a reactor meltdown was a distinct enough possibility that one member of the federal Nuclear Regulatory Commission was urging the evacuation of the surrounding Pennsylvania countryside.

I suspected our interview would be rescheduled, given the urgency of the day's events, but no. When I spoke with Leo Yochum, I mentioned that many observers believed that nuclear power was dead in the United States, especially now that Three Mile Island had intensified safety concerns. "I just don't understand this talk about nuclear being dead," Yochum replied, annoyance in his voice. "There is a nuclear imperative in this country. We know it, Wall Street knows it, and we're prepared to meet it."

Interviews like these convinced me that nothing the industry could say or do would surprise me. But GAP's investigations proved me wrong. Outlandish rhetoric is one thing, but GAP uncovered criminal behavior that put millions of lives at risk.

In May 1980 a private investigator named Tom Applegate came to GAP with explosive information concerning the Zimmer nuclear power plant, a massive facility under construction outside Cincinnati. The local electric utility, Cincinnati Gas & Electric Company, had hired Applegate to spy on workers the company suspected were cheating on their time cards. Applegate joined the workforce and discovered that some workers were indeed overstating the number of hours they worked. But he also came across genuinely alarming information. A number of critical safety welds had been inadequately completed and had cracked, he told a CG&E vice president. What's more, it appeared that a cover-up had been attempted: X-rays of the faulty welds had been doctored to make them appear sufficient.

"So Applegate went back to the [CG&E vice president] and told him this information," Devine recalls. "But little did [Applegate] know that the guy he was reporting to was the mastermind of the whole thing. The boss was trying to keep construction costs down and make Zimmer the cheapest nuclear plant in history. The VP told Applegate that he was fired and to keep his mouth shut or else. His exact words were, 'You're just a mouse, we are an elephant, we will crush you.'"

Devine sought out the chief welder at the Zimmer plant as the first step in his investigation. "He told me that while he wanted to kill Tom Applegate for ratting on him about the time cards, Tom was right about the welding being cracked and unsafe." As word spread of Devine's investigation and he gained the trust of one worker after another, more insiders came forward. Eventually, GAP assembled sworn statements from fifty whistle-blowers raising questions about the safety procedures at Zimmer. The sheer number created credibility problems for CG&E and the other companies trying to build the plant. "They might say the first person is lying, or even the fourth or fifth in line," says Devine. "By the time they say the fiftieth person is lying, [everyone] knows there is something going on."

The expanding roster of witnesses also handed Devine what every investigator dreams of: a trove of official documents proving that the alleged wrongdoing occurred. Like one half of an old married couple, Clark broke into fits of laughter as he recalled Devine's single-minded rapture. "At one point Tom flew to Cincinnati and ended up being given four boxes of original company documents—the original documents, not copies," Clark began. "There were seventy-six letters between Kaiser Engineering [one of the firms constructing the plant] and CG&E. Kaiser complained over and over again that CG&E wasn't budgeting enough money for quality assurance: they had only four inspectors when normally there would be about two hundred.

"Tom is so excited to get these documents that he doesn't pay attention on the drive back to the airport and the cops pull him over for speeding," Clark continued. "He doesn't have bail money, so the cops throw him in jail. Somehow, he talks the cops into letting him take his documents with him while he waits to get bailed out. A few hours later, I get the money wired out there and a colleague goes to bail him out. But Tom doesn't want to go—he's too busy studying the documents! When the cops come to his cell, Tom yells at them, 'Ten minutes! Just give me ten more minutes.'"

The document haul paved the way for a guerilla tactic GAP went on to use in countless other cases over the years—a tactic that Edward Snowden employed as well. "CG&E didn't know we had the documents," Clark recalled. "So when we began to make public statements alleging safety flaws and possible cover-ups at Zimmer, the company attacked us for making irresponsible accusations with no evidence. We led them right into the trap. They thought they had destroyed the evidence. But we disclosed in court that we obtained documents CG&E had claimed didn't exist, which exposed the company as a liar. I noticed Snowden did something similar. You release some damning stuff, and then wait for the government to try to bluster its way out. Then you release more documents showing that the government was lying yet again."

"We have been accused of hit and run tactics, to which I would proudly plead guilty," said Devine. "If we were to fight a corporation that has unlimited resources and just duke it out with them, there wouldn't be enough hours in the day to respond to all the motions that would be filed. So [we try to create] a situation in which they have to keep reacting to us, where they don't know what we're going to do next. We keep opening new fronts they have to devote resources to. There was a frustrated statement from the Nuclear Regulatory Commission towards the end of the Zimmer case that GAP keeps generating new allegations faster than we can put the old ones to rest. . . . That is the strategy of guerilla legal warfare: don't react to the power structure, let them react to us."

By the end of the Zimmer battle, GAP and its allies had not only forced the cancellation of an unsafe nuclear power plant that was 97 percent constructed—something that had never happened before—the group had developed what would be its modus operandi for years to come. In brief: hear what a potential whistle-blower has to say; investigate the allegations rigorously ("We're a small NGO going up against rich and powerful corporations," said Clark, "so we can't afford to be wrong"); counsel the potential whistle-blower on the likely consequences of speaking out, including losing one's job, being attacked in the media, and other forms of retaliation. If the whistle-blower still wants to go ahead, seek out journalists who might report the story. Accumulate safety in numbers by alerting relevant activists, civic groups, and other possible supporters about the whistle-blower's revelations. Then press Go.

Killing a multibillion dollar project that's nearly finished is the kind of thing that gets top management's attention. Especially when it happens twice.

At the very time GAP was fighting the Zimmer plant, it got drawn into a controversy over how to clean up the site of the Three Mile Island accident. In both cases, GAP found itself facing the Bechtel corporation, one of the most secretive, well-connected companies on earth. This was in the early 1980s, when President Ronald Reagan's cabinet included two former senior Bechtel executives: George Schultz, the secretary of state, and Caspar Weinberger, the secretary of defense. GAP whipped the giant company twice in a row; the *Wall Street Journal* estimated that GAP cost Bechtel $10 billion in construction delays, penalties, and foregone revenues.

At Three Mile Island, an engineer named Rick Parks warned GAP that, in Devine's words, "we were going to have a complete meltdown because [the cleanup] was being done so illegally and messily. The climax would be Bechtel's attempt to use a power crane to lift a 170-ton reactor vessel, which still contained smoldering radioactive rubble from the accident. Rick came to us four days before the lift was going to take place to say that the crane could fail because its electrical system had been damaged in the accident, but Bechtel wasn't willing to take the time to test whether the crane would work. Rick and I worked forty out of the next forty-eight hours and came up with a fifty-three-page affidavit that we took to Congress. Eventually, the NRC told Bechtel to start over on the cleanup, including doing load tests on the crane, and that the public wasn't going to pay for this second phase of work. The load tests failed a bunch of times, and even when they finally did carry the load, the crane froze in the air a number of times. I feel that without GAP the damage could have been incredibly extensive."

GAP's success in these David and Goliath battles carried a cost. The board of directors at the Institute for Policy Studies was advised that companies such as Bechtel could retaliate against GAP by suing IPS, GAP's parent organization. IPS's assets could be frozen until such a lawsuit was adjudicated, effectively shutting down the organization for years. The IPS board voted to spin GAP off before that scenario could unfold. "We sort of got tossed out," Clark recalled.

Chickens Bathed in "Fecal Soup"

The Government Accountability Project and I both left IPS in the same year, 1984. I went off to write a book about the press and the Reagan presidency, *On Bended Knee*; GAP established itself as an independent nonprofit organization. The forced departure was difficult for GAP in some ways, Clark recalled, but there were advantages. Disconnected from IPS and its left-of-center identity, GAP could pursue philanthropic support and political work with a broader ideological range of partners—in particular, Republican lawmakers such as Senator Grassley. With his conservative suspicion of government spending, Grassley was inclined to support whistle-blowers who could bring to light "waste, fraud and abuse" in government programs, but the senator from Iowa would look askance at IPS's condemnations of US imperialism and corporate greed.

GAP continued to be active in the nuclear field throughout the 1980s, but it also branched out and scored victories in other areas, exposing billions of dollars worth of Pentagon cost overruns and the illegal logging of publicly owned forests. I saw little of Devine and Clark in these years, but when I did, they updated me on their battles. The one I least enjoyed hearing about concerned the US poultry industry and the ghastly conditions its chickens experienced on their way to Americans' dinner tables.

GAP had whistle-blowers inside the US Department of Agriculture who charged that USDA, under pressure from the poultry industry, was allowing disgusting practices in slaughterhouses. Once chickens were killed, they were shuttled through an assembly line where workers and machines plucked, washed, and otherwise transformed the carcasses into the plastic encased products that eventually appeared in grocery stores. But along the way, the whistle-blowers said, the birds floated in wastewater so foul—thanks to remnants of blood and fecal matter removed from their lifeless bodies—that some inspectors referred to it as "fecal soup." For its part, industry insisted that the procedures posed no dangers and the inspectors were busybodies prone to exaggerating.

Not wanting to contemplate fecal soup for weeks on end, I wasn't even tempted to write about this story. But I did take notice when it ran on *60 Minutes*. In those days of pre-cable TV, *60 Minutes* was by far the most influential news program in the United States. It could make you a star, or ruin your life, in a single Sunday evening episode. The broadcast of March 29, 1987, featured correspondent Diane Sawyer narrating as follows:

"Tomorrow morning, if you buy a chicken at any supermarket, the chances are better than one in three that the chicken you pick out will be carrying bacteria called salmonella, which this year will kill hundreds of people and cause thousands more to come down with a kind of flu. . . . And what is the USDA doing about it? Well, we went to some of USDA's own employees to find out, and they told us that some chicken producers regularly violate health standards and that the USDA looks the other way."

The whistle-blower who led GAP into this investigation was Dr. Carl Telleen. A USDA employee since 1960, Telleen grew concerned about the potential spread of salmonella after USDA relaxed regulation of chicken processing in 1978. The industry had wanted permission to use new technology to remove chickens' innards, even though the new technology meant that carcasses still contaminated with fecal matter would merely be dunked in chlorinated water afterwards, not properly cleaned. When Telleen kept objecting to this practice, his superiors transferred him from Kansas to Washington, DC. Telleen, 65, suspected that the transfer was a veiled attempt to induce him to retire. Instead, he used his new posting in the nation's capital to spread his warning, à la Paul Revere, that salmonella was coming, salmonella was coming, unless the USDA changed course.

GAP and Telleen's revelations—especially once amplified by *60 Minutes*—led to wholesales changes in how Americans purchased and prepared chicken as well as substantial reforms in industry practices and government's regulation of same. Per usual, GAP collaborated with public interest groups and a range of news media outlets as part of its "strategic legal campaign." The response of workers in both the poultry industry and the USDA illustrated another emerging truth about GAP's mode of activism: the more whistle-blowers it publicized, the more whistle-blowers came forward. This virtuous circle eventually led GAP to represent some six hundred whistle-blowers in the poultry sector, enough to achieve a sizable public effect.

"We succeeded in getting several corrupt USDA managers forced out of their jobs," Devine later recalled. "That led to another wave of whistle-blowers. We got another bunch of plants shut down on the West Coast because there was so much filth. That led to more whistle-blowers in the Midwest who started to read about us through the trade journals. Then we had a piece on *60 Minutes* in the spring of 1987 and repeated that summer. That resulted in our doubling the number of statements from inspectors and workers. . . . These people are willing to take the risks, to stick their necks out to get this problem solved."

America's Palace Court Press

Years later, I worked with GAP whistle-blowers on one of the biggest journalist scoops of my career. Like Snowden and Drake's later exposés, this scoop also revolved around the 9/11 tragedy—specifically, the US government's shocking lack of preparedness against terrorist attacks. The scoop also schooled me on what I would come to recognize as a pattern:

most whistle-blowers first try to raise their concerns through official channels; they speak out publicly only after the system fails to respond, and then they face savage retaliation from that very system. "Whistle-blowers don't start out as dissidents," says Devine. "Usually, they are the ones who believe most strongly in the institution where they work. That's why they speak out—to help the institution live up to its mission. It's the indifference and retaliation from management many whistle-blowers face that can turn them into dissidents."

My scoop was published in *Vanity Fair*, in part because some of the stories told by GAP's whistle-blowers were not just frightening but freighted with a black humor that was undeniably entertaining.

For six years prior to 9/11, "red teams" of fake terrorists working for the Federal Aviation Administration (FAA) had tested US airport security by trying to sneak bombs and weapons onto commercial airline flights. According to Bogdan Dzakovic, a former security specialist on the FAA Red Team from 1995 to 2001, the fake terrorists succeeded more than eight times out of ten. Some of the worst security performances were at Ronald Reagan National Airport in Washington, DC, an airport often used by members of Congress and other senior government officials; security at Reagan National was breached 85 percent of the time during inspections in 1998.

One time, Dzakovic recalled, he and his colleagues "decided to push through an alarmed door and then wait around to get caught so we could see how the security system reacted." The Red Team agents took their positions, Dzakovic forced the door open, and the alarm started ringing. Thirty seconds passed, then a full minute. No airport security arrived. The alarm kept blaring as passengers strolled past. After fifteen minutes, the Red Team agents gave up in disgust.

Dzakovic and other Red Team members repeatedly warned their superiors that the United States was a sitting duck for terrorist attacks. But FAA officials buried the Red Team's reports, because, Dzakovic charged, the FAA was concerned more about keeping airplanes flying than about ensuring real security.

"The only thing that surprised me about September 11 was that it didn't happen sooner," Dzakovic told me. "The civilian-aviation security system was and remains basically an expensive façade. It makes the flying public think it's being protected—you know, all the theater of standing in line at airports and taking off your shoes—but it doesn't do much to deter serious terrorists."

Meanwhile, fake terrorists were also attacking the Los Alamos National Laboratory and other US nuclear weapons facilities. Located in the mountains of New Mexico, Los Alamos was the government's main facility for processing plutonium, the key ingredient in nuclear weapons. Rich Levernier, a war games specialist at the Department of Energy (which oversees the nuclear weapons program) was tasked with testing the facilities' preparedness against terrorist attacks.

Once a year, Levernier's mock-terrorist squads (made up of US military commandos) would assault Los Alamos. Neither side in these engagements shot real ammunition; harmless laser weapons were used. Nevertheless, the exercises were deadly serious. Levernier's attackers were ordered to penetrate the facility, capture its plutonium, and escape; the facility's security forces were expected to repel the mock attackers. "In more than 50 percent of our tests," Levernier told me, "we got in, captured the plutonium, got out again, and in some cases didn't fire a shot, because we didn't encounter any guards." To add insult to injury, in one war game Levernier's forces took the captured plutonium away in a Home Depot shopping cart.

This, despite the fact the Los Alamos security forces were told months in advance exactly what day the "terrorists" were coming.

Vanity Fair published my exposé in November 2003, a turn of events that illustrates another important but rarely acknowledged aspect of whistle-blowing in the United States: the difficulty of getting the nation's most powerful news organizations to publish or broadcast information that the government or other powerful interests do not want publicized.

Before I approached *Vanity Fair*, my article was rejected by two other top national magazines. Indeed, the article was spiked by the *New York Times Sunday Magazine*, even though the magazine's editors had approved my initial proposal to do the story and even flew me to Los Alamos to investigate the whistle-blowers' allegations firsthand. The *Times* magazine killed my article at the last minute, after I'd returned from Los Alamos, submitted my manuscript, and my immediate editor and I had revised it to where we were happy with it. That editor and I were waiting to hear whether the piece was going into the following week's issue or a future one when he emailed to say that the editor-in-chief had decided the story "didn't work." I was never told the reason, despite requesting an explanation.

Of course stories get killed all the time, sometimes for defensible reasons. But the fact that my article later appeared in *Vanity Fair*—as competitive a place to publish as then existed in the US news media—suggests that something else may have been to blame.

I believe that this episode illustrates another point of Snowden's: in the United States, the supposedly free,

independent, "liberal" press is often none of those things. The
New York Times and other large news organizations are more
linked with the government than not—more inclined to share,
or at least grant the benefit of the doubt to, the worldview and
policies of top government officials than to challenge them.

I don't make this argument on the basis of hearsay or personal pique. In the 1980s, I interviewed 175 White House
and news media officials for my book, *On Bended Knee: The
Press and the Reagan Presidency*, and I have freelanced for
mainstream media organizations and closely observed their
behavior throughout my career. I wish to emphasize that
there are many honorable journalists working inside the
mainstream media. But the institution as a whole follows
certain rules—rules that generally are unwritten but clearly
communicated by editors' decisions about which stories and
journalistic approaches get published and prioritized and
which do not.

The mainstream news media's unspoken definition of
responsible coverage of the government begins with this rule
of thumb: quote a government official whenever possible. It
further advises, in the name of balance, give equal time to both
major parties. Obviously, this latter directive has become less
true for overtly partisan outlets such as Fox on the right and
MSNBC on the left, but the larger point holds. Paul Krugman,
the Princeton University economics professor who doubles
as a *New York Times* columnist, has repeatedly skewered the
media's insistence on bipartisan balance and holding both
political parties equally to blame, even as the facts of a given
news story recommend no such "balanced" approach.

Further rules of thumb: downplay or ignore information and points of view that come from outside the centers
of political and economic power. Rely all but exclusively on
the opposition party to provide any critical comment of the

government; if the opposition party largely agrees with the government on the matter at hand, so will most mainstream news coverage. Thus mainstream coverage largely reflects how the dominant sectors of the Democratic and Republican parties in Washington define a given issue, no matter how much this framing might contradict verifiable facts or common sense.

This approach to journalism skews mainstream media coverage in at least two ways: First, the coverage of any president is only as critical as the opposition party chooses to be; and second, coverage of specific issues reflects not so much reality as what the two major political parties *say* is reality. Thus both Ronald Reagan and George W. Bush, since they faced opposition parties that were rarely aggressive, faced relatively little negative coverage. By contrast, George H. W. Bush and especially Bill Clinton and Barack Obama encountered much tougher coverage thanks to the harsh, relentless criticism they faced from the opposition parties during *their* administrations.

As for the coverage of specific issues, David Hoffman, a White House correspondent for the *Washington Post*, pointed to Reagan's doubling of the military budget—and the Democrats' refusal to object—as "the perfect example" of how the press accepts the Washington establishment's spectrum of debate rather than presenting independent analysis. "We fill the paper with stories on the margin of issues, not sweeping overviews," Hoffman told me. "If you went through the paper and stamped every story whether it was 2 degrees, 5 degrees or 360 degrees [off the center of the debate], you would see a lot of 2 degree stories."

In the Reagan years, this tendency of the mainstream media to act as a stenographer to power meant that Reagan's characterization of Central American death squads as "freedom fighters" went largely unchallenged, just as President Bill Clinton's subsequent claims that financial deregulation was a win for bankers and consumers alike escaped critical scrutiny. This same tendency helped the Bush-Cheney administration drive the nation to attack Iraq in the name of eliminating "weapons of mass destruction" that turned out not to exist (just as many outside critics alleged). Likewise, it shielded President Obama (and the Congress) from sustained criticism of the bailout of Wall Street bankers but not of the millions of average homeowners the bankers damaged following the 2008 financial crash.

In short, mainstream US news organizations tend to function like a palace court press. As key members of the palace court society known as official Washington, their coverage reflects the points of view held by the powers that be instead of providing an independent picture. To the rest of us, the sky may be blue and the grass green, but unless powerful figures within the palace court affirm it, you won't hear that from the Washington press corps.

"Hiding That Story Changed History"

But isn't the *New York Times* an exception, given that it published the Pentagon Papers? And the first authoritative account of the Bush-Cheney administration's warrantless surveillance programs? And any number of other stories that challenge Washington policies?

Perhaps, but it is only a partial exception. If you plumb the history of the *New York Times* and the centers of political power, you find all too often a cozy relationship. The picture that emerges is one of great hesitance if not reluctance on the part of senior *Times* executives to challenge what the president of the United States and top aides claim is true.

Ellsberg relates this story in his memoir, *Secrets*, making clear that while the newspaper did the journalistically correct thing in the end—defying Nixon's threats and publishing the Pentagon Papers—it was a close call.

For his part, Snowden was appalled by the backstory to the *Times* December 2005 article on warrantless surveillance; he later cited it as a primary reason why he favored Poitras and Greenwald rather than the *Times* with the documents he secreted out of the NSA. Snowden knew that the *Times* reporters who uncovered that December 2005 story, James Risen and Eric Lichtblau, had in fact completed their article and submitted it to their editors in autumn 2004— weeks *before* Bush's 2004 bid for re-election and more than a year before the editors at last published it. Furthermore, *Times* editors ran the piece in December 2005 only after Risen called their bluff by saying that he was going to break the scoop himself in his forthcoming book, *State of War*.

"Hiding that story changed history," Snowden told Greenwald. Correctly or not, Snowden believed that if the *Times* had published the Risen-Lichtblau article before the 2004 election, its revelations about Bush and Cheney's warrantless surveillance could have sparked enough public displeasure to perhaps cost the president and vice president the election. Thus Snowden decided to pass the NSA documents to two independent journalists rather than to the most powerful newspaper in the world. In effect, Snowden concluded that the *New York Times* of 2013 was no longer the *Times* that had published the Pentagon Papers in 1971 and could not be trusted to do justice to the story Snowden was risking his life to expose.

A news outlet as powerful as the *Times* can change history not only by hiding stories but also by mistakenly hyping them. One of the most shameful episodes centered on the *Times'* relentless championing of claims that Iraqi dictator Saddam Hussein possessed "weapons of mass destruction" and therefore had to be overthrown before he could use them. *Times* reporter Judith Miller wrote many of these stories, relying on information provided by Ahmad Chalabi and other Iraqi exiles eager for Hussein's ouster, even as she ignored or disparaged copious evidence to the contrary.

Much of Miller's published information was inaccurate, as the *Times* finally admitted in an Editor's Note in 2004. By then, however, the colossal damage had been done. The United States was mired in a war that still is creating chaos and casualties in the region. During the tension-filled run-up to the disastrous invasion of Iraq, Miller's bogus stories—appearing on the front page of America's most influential newspaper—helped sway elite opinion, shape the coverage provided by the rest of the media, and build the case for war. Notwithstanding their disdain for the supposedly liberal press, Bush-Cheney administration officials frequently cited the *Times'* articles to bolster their arguments for invading Iraq. After all, if even "liberals" were saying Saddam had weapons of mass destruction, it had to be true, right?

Nor was the *Times* alone in its deference to government power, in Snowden's view. "After 9/11," he said, "many of the most important news outlets in America abdicated their role as a check to power—the journalistic responsibility to challenge the excesses of government—for fear of being seen as unpatriotic and punished in the market during a period of heightened nationalism."

It made sense, then, that Snowden's disclosures appeared first in a British, rather than an American, news outlet. Further, it made sense that the *Guardian* was the outlet in question, for the newspaper had a long, distinguished history of aggressively challenging the powers that be in many spheres. And as a newspaper of the left, the *Guardian* was comfortable criticizing not only the administration of right-wingers George W. Bush and Dick Cheney but also that of center-leftist Barack Obama.

There are, however, exceptions to the American media's usual posture of deference, which is how my article on GAP's nuclear and airline security whistle-blowers eventually came to appear in *Vanity Fair*. Graydon Carter, the magazine's editor, was by no means cavalier about the terrorist threat; he and his family lived only a few blocks from the former site of the World Trade Center. As a responsible editor should, he had my article vetted by outside experts. And while Carter's *Vanity Fair* devoted most of its pages to celebrating the rich and famous, he was one of the few senior mainstream editors who did not buckle beneath the intimidating political climate fostered by the Bush-Cheney administration in the wake of 9/11. Once Carter was satisfied that my article did not unwittingly provide information useful to terrorists, he didn't hesitate; he published.

Which is what a free and independent press is supposed to do. The press's responsibility within America's constitutional system is to inform the public and cast a probing eye on what the government of the day is doing, even when—especially when—that government may not appreciate it.

"It's Ruined My Life"

Interviewing the whistle-blowers I met through the *Vanity Fair* exposé and other journalistic investigations has given me some insights into what makes whistle-blowers tick. Whistle-blowers come in various personality types, but virtually all of them are compelled by a powerful sense of individual responsibility. They often see life as a series of moral choices, and their consciences will not allow them to cut corners, despite the evident risks. Thus Snowden, Wigand, and numerous other whistle-blowers reject descriptions of them as heroes, insisting that they are ordinary people who simply had a responsibility and fulfilled it.

"I have values that just won't let me participate in illegal things," one whistle-blower at the federal General Services Administration told GAP's Devine. "There is nothing extraordinary about me at all. I'm no hero. But you've got to live with yourself. If I didn't [speak out], how could I live with that face in the mirror every morning?"

"There are different kinds of whistle-blowers," said Edwards of GAP. "There is the zealot, who is the trickiest to handle but also pretty rare. There are the accidental ones who don't know they blew the whistle; they just know that everything went to hell all of a sudden. There's the kind who goes along with wrongdoing and tries to ignore it, but then realizes they can't stomach it and have to speak out. And there are the straight arrow types who say, 'I was just doing my job.' They're often law enforcement types."

Thomas Drake plainly belonged in the straight arrow category, as did Rich Levernier, the guy whose mock-terrorist squads made a dark joke of security protections at Los Alamos. Levernier emphasized in our interviews that he was a decidedly involuntary whistle-blower. A twenty-two-year veteran of the Department of Energy who had previously served nine years as an Army intelligence officer, he was by his own admission not someone who usually questioned authority. Working through the established bureaucratic channels, he tried for years to get his superiors at DOE to address the shortcomings that his war games had identified. But most of those superiors, he said, declined to acknowledge that the problems even existed, much less needed fixing.

Also like Drake, Levernier was a by-the-book kind of guy with a serious if not stern demeanor. He related his story to me poker-faced, in an urgent monotone. Devine said it took six months of working together before he got Levernier to crack a smile. "Rich reminds me of Joe Friday in *Dragnet*," Devine said. "Actually, he makes Joe seem animated."

One year, Levernier gave up his Super Bowl Sunday to run a surprise spot check on the security forces at the Rocky Flats nuclear facility near Denver. He and a colleague discovered that "patrols that were required three times per hour were not seen for more than six hours." He and the colleague went looking for the absentees and found the entire squad inside, watching the football game.

Chris Steele, another whistle-blower at Los Alamos, likewise was a personal eccentric who held his staff to exacting standards. As DOE's senior safety official on site, Steele was responsible for making sure that the lab's operations did not put workers, the public, or the environment at undue risk. A self-described nerdy workaholic, he was stumped when I asked what he did for fun. "I'm kind of boring," he said with a shrug before mentioning that he spent his last vacation recalculating radiation releases from a hypothetical accident at Los Alamos.

Nor did Steele suffer fools gladly. "Retarded" and "moron" were but two of the politically incorrect words he used for colleagues whose work did not measure up. He vetoed numerous proposals he regarded as dangerous, illegal, or just plain wacky. In 1998 he overruled a Los Alamos scientist who was so determined to run a certain experiment that he offered to drive a bulldozer into a nuclear reactor if the reactor overheated during the experiment. "I told him that was maybe the bravest thing I'd ever heard," Steele dryly recalled, "because he'd certainly be killed by the radiation. But it wasn't much of a plan."

Levernier and Steele shared another trait, one found among many whistle-blowers: a persistent, almost naïve determination to continue raising their concerns until the underlying problems were addressed. Whistle-blowers take the system at its word, confronting colleagues and superiors with well-documented objections, demanding answers, and then they seem almost shocked when their entreaties are rebuffed and they end up in hot water: surely everyone else should care as much as they do about making things right, shouldn't they?

Even then, many of these whistle-blowers keep coming, refusing to back down, and in many cases end up paying a steep price. Both Steele and Levernier, like Drake years later, were stripped of their security clearances, and therefore their professions, after coming forward with claims of wrongdoing and then sticking to their guns in the face of hostility from higher-ups.

With GAP's assistance, Steele successfully fought back and was reinstated, but Levernier's story had no such happy ending. The war games specialist was not fired outright—that could have given him due process rights—but revoking his clearance effectively ended his career two years before he was due to retire with a full pension. He was then transferred to an administrative job at DOE even as his reputation was ruined by a whisper campaign charging, falsely, that he had leaked classified information. "When I walk down the halls now," he said, "people I have known for twenty-five years turn and walk away. The stink they put on me is so strong that no one with any career aspirations wants to get close to me.

"If I had to do this over again, I wouldn't," Levernier said. "I would have been more aggressive about keeping a record of the shortcomings I witnessed, and I'd have laid it on my bosses' doorsteps, and then if they didn't do anything, that failure would be on their backs. But that's all. Because now I recognize that the power your superiors have over you is broad and deep, and they don't hesitate to use it. When they took my security clearance, it was like a scarlet letter was painted on my forehead. It's ruined my life."

"How Can We Fix It?"

With their unswerving moral compasses and strict adherence to rules and regulations, whistle-blowers aren't always the easiest persons to work with, a fact that can work against them when the targets of their disclosures fight back. The retaliation they encounter can in turn kindle feelings of paranoia, distrust, self-pity, and depression that go beyond the economic punishment of losing one's job. Whistle-blowers can become so obsessive in the quest for justice that they drive even allies, including the attorneys at GAP, crazy.

Devine blamed the break-up of his marriage in part on middle-of-the-night phone calls he got for months on end from Aldric Saucier, the US Army scientist whose revelations about faked test results for the "Star Wars" missile defense program helped kill what Saucier contended was a $1 trillion boondoggle. "He never left my family alone," Devine recalled. Yet Devine confessed that he "kept taking his calls" not just because Devine was more than a bit obsessive himself, but also because Saucier sometimes faced undeniably urgent situations, such as the night two thugs badly beat him outside his home in suburban Virginia.

Physical attacks, though rare, are but one in a suite of retaliatory tactics bureaucracies routinely employ against whistle-blowers, Devine added. "Shooting the messenger" is the cornerstone of the bureaucratic response, he said. His book provides a list of the subsidiary tactics most commonly employed toward that end; the list is adapted from the Malek Manual, a secret report president Nixon commissioned on "how to purge the career civil service system of 'unresponsive' employees—whistle-blowers or Democrats—without running afoul of the law," wrote Devine, who noted the irony that the Malek Manual was itself exposed by federal whistle-blowers.

"The first imperative of retaliation is to make the whistleblower the issue: obfuscate the dissent by attacking the source's motives, credibility, professional competence or virtually anything else that will work to cloud the issue," Devine continued. "The point is to direct the spotlight at the whistleblower instead of the alleged misconduct." For example, superiors of Steele and Levernier repeatedly complained that the two whistle-blowers' personalities and their refusal to be "team players" were the reasons for stripping their security clearances, not the men's challenges of institutional practices. (One of Levernier's staff derided the superiors' assertions, asking of Levernier, "Did he have a pleasing personality? I didn't have to marry the guy, so that wasn't my problem. But to say he wasn't a team player is a bum rap. What that means is, 'Don't bring us any bad news, because we don't want to deal with the problems.'")

Daniel Ellsberg was likewise derided as a malcontent and glory seeker after he leaked the Pentagon Papers. He was also targeted for physical attack, he later claimed; citing information he received from a prosecutor in the Watergate scandal, Ellsberg said that the White House Plumbers hired a group of thugs to "totally incapacitate" him at an antiwar rally, but Ellsberg eluded them. Many observers have speculated that the Plumbers' break-in of Ellsberg's psychiatrist's office was aimed at digging up dirt that could be publicized to smear Ellsberg as anti-American or simply a lunatic.

Ellsberg believes there was another motive: "They wanted to keep me from leaking additional information," he told me. "The break-in was partly about damaging my reputation, but mainly it was to threaten me into shutting up about what their Vietnam policy actually was."

The dubiousness of blaming the messenger is clear when one considers perhaps the most famous, if anonymous, whistle-blower in history: the "Deep Throat" of Watergate. "Whistle-blowers can have mixed motives, but it doesn't mean they're wrong," argued GAP's Edwards. "The primary example is Mark Felt, the main whistleblower behind the Watergate scandal." Felt, who was famously nicknamed "Deep Throat" by *Washington Post* reporters Bob Woodward and Carl Bernstein, "was pissed off," Edwards continues, "because [FBI director J. Edgar] Hoover passed him over for promotion at the FBI. His disclosure came from what amounted to a personnel dispute. But it showed that the president was operating illegally and that was certainly in the public interest to reveal."

Snowden, too, got the "shoot the messenger" treatment—he was denigrated as a high school drop-out, a bureaucratic grunt with dreams of grandeur, a traitor intent on selling US secrets to China and Russia, and more—but he blunted such attacks through a series of proactive maneuvers that once again set him apart from most whistle-blowers, not to mention demonstrated his shrewd understanding of how media and image making operated in today's world.

Above all, Snowden took steps in advance to *define himself* in the eyes of the public, rather than letting the media and government do the defining. He achieved this primarily by taping a video interview with Laura Poitras that identified him as the leaker of the NSA documents and gave his reasons for doing so; the video was posted on the *Guardian* website with the newspaper's first NSA scoops. From there, other news outlets quickly picked it up and spread it through their networks, exponentially increasing its reach and influence. The public therefore was introduced to Snowden not as an anonymous character being led away in handcuffs—as had been the case with Drake—but rather as a calm, well-spoken, professionally dressed young man who clearly had thought carefully about what he was doing and was prepared to pay a price for his decision. In short, he came across as a person of conscience, not a shifty-eyed traitor.

Poitras and Glenn Greenwald, aided by MacAskill of the *Guardian*, were vital allies in establishing Snowden's public persona. Poitras shot the video in a flattering but authoritative tone and melded Snowden's revelations with just enough personal insights to humanize the man. Greenwald, a lawyer turned journalist, was a ferocious advocate for Snowden, especially in the days following the initial revelations when Snowden was in limbo inside the Moscow airport and unable to speak for himself. Some mainstream journalists sounded as critical of Snowden as government officials were; Greenwald blasted them as government toadies who had forgotten that journalists were supposed to welcome the disclosure of newsworthy information. For example, Jeffrey Toobin, a legal analyst for CNN and the *New Yorker*, defended the NSA's warrantless surveillance as a "legally authorized" program, called Snowden "a grandiose narcissist who deserves to be in prison," and condemned him for fleeing to China and then Russia. Greenwald shot back that one reason Snowden left the United States before leaking the documents was that it was "a country full of Jeffrey Toobins" who would throw him in jail rather than confront his disclosures.

The battle over how the public would judge Snowden would continue for years—it continues still—and his critics unleashed plenty of firepower. But this initial public relations maneuver asserting control over his own image and message, augmented by Snowden's continued willingness to do interviews and public appearances (via satellite) to explain his actions, made it much harder to "shoot the messenger" or discredit him in the way many previous whistle-blowers had been.

Time and again, Snowden told audiences, he did what he did out of a sense of responsibility and moral calling. In this respect, he was utterly typical of his newfound tribe. Responsibility is something whistle-blowers talk about a lot; it's perhaps the main reason they do what they do. Snowden apparently was not the only one among his colleagues who was disturbed by the NSA's mass surveillance—his day-to-day colleagues, he said, were "good people"—but he concluded he had the least to lose by revealing the information. Ray McGovern, the retired CIA agent who later befriended Snowden, recalled Snowden explaining his thought process. "Ed told me, 'I looked around the office one day, and one colleague had kids in college, another had a mortgage, another had elderly parents who needed looking after, and I realized, if someone is going to do this, it has to be me,'" McGovern told me.

"Whistle-blowers have a broader sense of empathy than the average person and they're guided by a sense of morality they can't just put on a shelf," said GAP's Clark. "They also have a capacity to identify with the *victims* of the information they're disclosing, whether it's the people being spied on in Snowden's case or the fleeced taxpayers Ernie Fitzgerald spoke up for in the 1960s. Whistle-blowers are also unique in that their morality doesn't change with circumstance. They don't say, 'Oh, I have an obligation to support my family, so I can't put that at risk by speaking out.' They don't see their family obligations as necessarily higher than their obligations to the society around them."

Indeed, the absolutism of some whistle-blowers' moral calculus—Ellsberg was a striking example—led them to marvel that not everyone was willing to act the way they did. "Forty years passed after the Pentagon Papers and I had come to despair that anyone else would do anything like that," Ellsberg told me. "Then came Chelsea Manning with her revelations to Wikileaks about US atrocities in Iraq and three years later Snowden. So in all those years you've got three people who've spoken out, despite the fact that there are thousands who could have done it. Remember, what Snowden revealed was known by a thousand other insiders who also held the kind of super clearances Snowden did. Many of them hated and opposed [the NSA's mass surveillance]. But they had wives and mortgages and children going to college and they didn't speak out. Now, my own psychology leads me to ask, 'Why are there so few? Why are there are only three of us?'"

Here again, Snowden evinced wisdom beyond his years. When Ellsberg asked him much the same question during a joint appearance at the Hope X Conference in July 2014, Snowden replied that he would rather focus on encouragement than condemnation. "I don't want to take a negative stance in judging [those who remain silent] and say, 'You didn't do what you were supposed to do, you didn't do what you swore you would do,'" Snowden said. "Even if that is the case, I think of it from an engineer's perspective and go, 'How can we fix it?'"

Though barely in his thirties, Snowden came across as an old soul who was gentle in demeanor but unswerving in determination. The goal, he said, should be to empower whistle-blowers and improve transparency such that, when governments around the world "do unlawful things, when they do unconstitutional things, or when they do things that are entirely legal but comprehensively immoral, we will find out about it. That will change the world."

PART THREE

The Third Man

"Do the Right Thing"

Growing up, John Crane spent his summers in Germany, where he heard countless times about the time his grandfather faced down Adolf Hitler at gunpoint. His mother and grandmother both told the story, and the moral never changed. "My family had been very involved in the anti-fascist opposition, so I was raised that you always try to do the right thing," Crane recalled. "And should someone do the right thing, there can of course be consequences."

Standing up to Hitler at gunpoint was a pretty high standard for a boy to live up to, but the moral lesson stayed with Crane as an adult, and decades later he became a formidable behind-the-scenes defender of Thomas Drake and other US government whistle-blowers. Crane was an assistant inspector general in the Department of Defense whose duties included supervising the whistle-blower unit. He worked to get Drake and the four officials Drake joined in blowing the whistle—former NSA executives William Binney, Kirk Wiebe, and Edward Loomis and former House of Representatives Permanent Select Committee on Intelligence staffer Diane Roark—a fair hearing and protection from retaliation. "I had no opinion on whether [Drake] was innocent or not, I was trying to make the system work as it's supposed to work," Crane told me.

But as his mother warned, there were consequences to trying to do the right thing, and in the end his bureaucratic superiors thwarted Crane. To his horror, Crane watched as Drake and the four other NSA whistle-blowers were secretly ratted out to the Justice Department and then had their homes raided at gunpoint by federal agents. Of the five members in this group, which I shall call the NSA 4+1, Drake fared the worst. As described in Part One of this book, he was stripped of his security clearance, indicted, threatened with life in prison, deprived of his federal pension, blackballed in security circles, and reduced to working as a clerk at an Apple store.

Crane's testimony, published here for the first time, sheds fresh light not only on Drake's persecution but also on the much better known whistle-blowing of Edward Snowden. "Crane was our fly on the wall, letting us understand after the fact what really happened to Drake," said Tom Devine of GAP, which represented both Crane and Drake as well as Snowden. Crane's account illuminates how a system that in theory is supposed to protect whistle-blowing can in practice do just the opposite, a lesson Snowden took to heart when planning his own disclosures.

For Drake, despite following official procedures for blowing the whistle on waste, fraud, or abuse, was ruthlessly punished and his concerns about constitutionally questionable surveillance were disregarded. Snowden therefore chose a different path: "civil disobedience whistle-blowing," as Devine dubbed it. Instead of approaching his superiors at the NSA or the congressional overseers of the agency, Snowden bypassed a system he concluded was corrupt and passed secret documents to journalists Laura Poitras, Glenn Greenwald, and Ewen MacAskill in June 2013.

But what actually happened to Drake inside the national security apparatus was more complicated than Snowden or any other outsider realized. Crane's testimony reveals that Drake in fact had defenders inside the system who insisted that proper procedures be followed—and who faced punishment themselves as a result.

"Without Thomas Drake," Snowden has said, "there would have been no Edward Snowden." But Crane's story suggests that there is another link in the chain. Had John Crane succeeded in making the Pentagon's whistle-blowing system function as advertised, Drake might not have become a foreboding example to Snowden of how *not* to blow the whistle. In other words, had Crane and Drake's intertwined story ended differently, Snowden might never have chosen civil disobedience whistle-blowing in the first place.

Crane, a solidly built Virginia resident with flecks of gray in a neatly trimmed chinstrap beard, understood why Snowden made the choice he did but still lamented it. "I think it's sad that someone finds himself in exile in a foreign country because he felt he couldn't use the various channels available to him," he said. "Someone like Snowden should not have felt the need to harm himself just to do the right thing."

"In This Way You Will Never Liberate Germany"

John Crane's grandfather was a few days shy of turning forty the night Hitler tried to take over Germany the first time. It was November 8, 1923, the night of the "Beer Hall Putsch." Plotting to overthrow the Weimar Republic, Hitler and some six hundred armed members of his fledgling Nazi party surrounded a beer hall in Munich where the governor of Bavaria, Gustav von Kahr, was addressing a large crowd. The rebels burst into the hall, planning to kidnap von Kahr and march on Berlin. Hitler fired his pistol in the air and shouted, in the frenzied voice that later would hurl Germany and the world into a nightmare of hatred and war, "The national revolution has begun!"

Crane's grandfather, Gustav Rudel, was in the beer hall as part of his military duties, Rudel later wrote in an eight-page, single-spaced affidavit that provided a minute-by-minute eyewitness account of the putsch. (Rudel later testified at the trial that sentenced Hitler to five years in prison.) The son of a prominent German general, Rudel had served with distinction in World War I, earning two Iron Crosses. By 1923, he had risen to the rank of captain in the army of the Weimar Republic. In Munich, he served as the chief political aide to General Otto von Lossow, the national army's highest ranking official in Bavaria; as such, Rudel was the chief liaison between von Lossow and von Kahr and thus privy to the two men's many dealings with Hitler.

Suspecting that Hitler and his followers were planning a coup, General Lossow and the head of Bavaria's state police, Colonel Hans Ritter von Seisser, forced their way into the beer hall to monitor developments. Rudel and Seisser's bodyguard were standing next to their bosses, listening to von Kahr address the crowd, when the doors to the hall were thrown open and a mass of armed men burst in, Hitler in the lead, while a previously hidden machine gun was unveiled in the upstairs gallery.

"Hitler, with pistol held high, escorted on right and left by armed men, his tunic stained with beer, stormed through the hall towards the podium," Rudel wrote in his affidavit. "When he was directly in front of us, police chief von Seisser's adjutant gripped [but did not draw] his sword. Hitler immediately aimed his pistol at the man's chest. I shouted, 'Mr. Hitler, in this way you will never liberate Germany.' Hitler hesitated, lowered his pistol and pushed his way between us to the podium."

In the surrounding chaos, Hitler's forces tried to force von Kahr, Lossow, and Seisser to join the coup, but the uprising soon fizzled. Foreshadowing the military ineptness he would display as Führer, Hitler left the beer hall to deal with a separate crisis, allowing von Kahr, von Lossow, von Seisser, and their aides to flee the building. Outside, the men sped off to alert the national army and local police. When Hitler's forces marched on the defense ministry, they were attacked and easily defeated. Hitler escaped but was arrested two days later.

Rudel and Hitler, however, were not finished with one another, and the years to come posed moral quandaries for Rudel that would be familiar to whistle-blowers of today: how does one balance one's loyalty to a flawed institution with one's personal conscience?

Rudel, a career military man, did not leave the German armed forces after Hitler came to power a decade later, despite what Crane described as his grandfather's antipathy to the rising despot. Why not? The family history as recounted by Crane offers a forgiving portrayal of Rudel's actions: his grandfather "remained loyal to the military as an institution,"

Crane told me. What's more, Rudel supposedly "tendered his resignation several times, but it wasn't accepted."

Yet Rudel presumably still could have chosen to walk away—the fact is, he did not. Instead, he rose through the ranks to the exalted position of commander of Germany's air defenses during the first two years of World War II. He was promoted to four-star general, partly on the strength of having helped to invent the .88 howitzer, an antiaircraft gun regarded as one of the most important innovations in twentieth century warfare. Crane maintained that "Lots of the senior officers were anti-fascist. They saw themselves as a constructive bulwark against Hitler's insanity." Yet that insanity could not have flourished without the participation of military men like Rudel, who, whatever their private qualms, continued to follow orders.

In any case, Hitler apparently never fully trusted Rudel, and the feeling was more than mutual. "As Führer, Hitler called most of his senior military officers by their names," said Crane. "My grandfather was the only one he didn't. The other commanders always remarked on it. To Hitler, my grandfather was always, Herr General—Mr. General." Hitler relieved Rudel of his command in 1942—"when Hitler thought he had the war won," says Crane. Fearing the worst, Rudel secretly moved himself and his family into a Catholic rectory in the countryside outside Munich to live out the rest of the war.

Regardless of his grandfather's morally ambiguous record, it was his courage in standing up to Hitler on the night of the Beer Hall Putsch that would inspire Crane nearly a half-century later when he faced his own moment of truth. Like the flutter of butterfly's wings can trigger unpredictable effects halfway around the world, so Rudel's act of courage reverberated across time, fortifying his grandson to persist in a ferocious behind-the-scenes battler over how the Pentagon should deal with whistle-blowers such as Drake and Snowden.

"We Were the Guys in White Hats"

Crane's father, an American, met his mother while studying in Germany after the war. Three children later (Crane has an older sister and an identical twin brother), the family moved to the States, where his father attended Harvard Law School. Crane grew up in the suburbs of Washington, DC, attending James Madison High School in Virginia, a regular American kid except that he spoke both German and English at home. His father was an intellectual by temperament, a Republican by politics. He worked as an intelligence analyst in the Nixon State Department and later joined the conservative Center for Strategic and International Studies.

When it came time for Crane to launch his career, the apple didn't fall far from the tree. He worked in Washington for a nongovernmental organization analyzing military issues and spent three years on Capitol Hill as a press aide to Republican members of Congress. In 1988, he was hired at the Inspector General's office of the Department of Defense.

The job seemed a good fit for Crane's idealism. In response to the Nixon administration's attempts to politicize the federal workforce, Congress had passed the Inspector General Act of 1978, creating the post of inspector general at twelve federal agencies. By 2016, the number of agencies with an IG, as the post was known in government, had risen to thirty-six. (Some local and state governments as well as private companies also had inspectors general.) The inspector general was a kind of internal judge and police chief, charged with making sure that a given agency was operating according to the law—obeying and enforcing rules and regulations, spending money efficiently and as authorized by Congress.

So the office of Inspector General was a logical place to house a whistle-blower unit. Beginning with the Whistle-blower Protection Act of 1989, federal employees had been encouraged to file whistle-blower complaints if they witnessed a violation of law, a gross waste of money, a gross abuse of authority, or a "substantial and specific" danger to public health or safety. The law promised protection for those who came forward: whistle-blowers' identities were to be kept secret, and whistle-blowers could not be demoted, fired, or otherwise punished for speaking out. The bill's cosponsor, Republican Senator Charles Grassley of Iowa, explained that "Under the current system, the vast majority of employees choose not to disclose the wrongdoing they see. They are afraid of reprisals, and the result is a gross waste of taxpayers' dollars. Government employers should not be allowed to cover up their misdeeds by creating such a hostile environment."

By 2004 Crane had been promoted to assistant inspector general. As such, he oversaw all of the Pentagon's whistle-blower investigation and protection functions. "In the IG's office, we were the guys with the white hats," Crane said. "We did what we did to have transparency encouraged, to let senior leadership know when there were problems that needed to be addressed and to make the larger [Defense Department] organization adhere to the rules and laws passed by Congress."

Crane took the sanctity of whistle-blower protection so seriously that he routinely carried around in his breast pocket a copy of the US Declaration of Independence and the Constitution as well as a booklet containing a copy of the 1978 Whistleblower Protection Act. "I had the booklet printed up so employees in the Inspector General's office could read the Act they were responsible for enforcing," he told me.

In December 2004, nine months after Crane began heading the Pentagon's whistle-blower office, the office issued a classified report on their investigation of the NSA 4+1's complaint. Fearing retaliation, Drake had requested that he not be named in the report; instead, he was identified as "a senior NSA executive." The other four whistle-blowers—Binney, Wiebe, Loomis, and Roark—had already retired from federal service and therefore were less concerned about retaliation, though by law their identities too were supposed to be kept confidential.

The NSA 4+1's whistle-blowing put them in direct conflict with Michael Hayden, the NSA director, and indirectly challenged the Bush-Cheney administration's larger approach to surveillance and counterterrorism policy. Following procedure, the NSA 4+1 filed their first whistle-blower complaint with the Inspector General of the NSA. The complaint raised two main points.

The first: Hayden and NSA's senior management had backed a new surveillance system to collect and analyze telephone, email, and other electronic communications, code-named Trailblazer, that was grotesquely overpriced. Trailblazer, the whistle-blowers charged, was a $3.8 billion boondoggle, more effective at channeling taxpayer dollars to corporate contractors than at protecting the homeland. Furthermore, they argued, Hayden and his aides had chosen Trailblazer even though an alternative system, code-named Thin Thread, which Binney had developed, had been shown to collect the desired information at a fraction of the cost.

"It's all run by money," Binney, 74, told me, the fury in his voice still palpable more than a decade later. He added,

"Hayden said recently that Thin Thread did not work, which was a lie. We had this program running at three separate sites, including one in Germany. But the contractors and Hayden wanted to kill it because it would have removed the justification for their Trailblazer program. The contractors were making $340/hour, which works out to almost $700,000 a year. They were lobbying to get us out of there—Booz Allen, Boeing, all the corporations up and down the National Business Parkway [the highway near NSA headquarters in Fort Meade, Maryland]—because if we used Thin Thread, they wouldn't get their big paychecks."

The second objection: Trailblazer made the United States, paradoxically, less secure. Trailblazer collected so much raw data, the NSA 4+1 argued, that NSA analysts were overwhelmed: they struggled to distinguish the genuinely important from the trivial and ended up missing vital clues (as Drake later charged regarding the San Diego hijackers and the 9/11 attacks, as described in Part One of this book). "What's really going on here, and NSA is trying to bury it, is that the analysts have too much data and they can't really tell what's going on," Binney told me.

Joel Brenner, the NSA's Inspector General from April 2002 until September 2006, ruled against the NSA 4+1's whistle-blower complaint and defended the propriety of his actions. "My office examined the adequacy of the selection process [for Trailblazer] and did not find it deficient," Brenner told me. "There were vehement disagreements within the Agency about the merits of the two approaches . . . but it was not the IG's role to second-guess a management decision when management had made a reasoned business judgment. The IG doesn't get to say, 'Well, General, you may have decided to do it this way, but if I had been in your shoes, I'd have done it differently.' The decision-maker has to make a record that the law was followed, alternatives were considered, and a reasoned decision was made. The Agency did that."

"I truly tire of this issue," Hayden told me in response to Binney's accusations. Regarding Thin Thread, he added, "We tried it. It had its performance challenges. And it wouldn't scale. We did fold elements of it into other modernization programs. NSA has its faults. Rejecting good technical solutions is not one of them. . . . Please note that [Thin Thread] was NOT the program of record when I arrived [at NSA], I did NOT make it the program of record, and neither did my successor. Hmm. Wonder why?"

Brenner went out of his way to say that he disagreed with how Drake was later retaliated against. "I don't approve of what Drake did [by talking to the press], but he was grossly over-prosecuted," Brenner said. "His infraction should have been dealt with as a misdemeanor or even administratively. Prosecuting him as a spy was unjust. . . . Decisions like that undermine the credibility of espionage prosecutions when they're really warranted. They also turn people who disagreed with their government into enemies of their government, which is tragic in the deep sense of the term."

After Brenner ruled against their complaint, the NSA 4+1 went up the bureaucratic ladder, filing the same complaint with the Department of Defense Office of Inspector General. There, Crane and his staff came to almost the exact opposite conclusion Brenner's office had: they "substantially affirmed" the two claims summarized above, Crane told me. What's more, they also affirmed a third allegation, one that only took shape during their interviews with the NSA 4+1— and that would leap to the fore of public discussion when Snowden went public in 2013.

The Trailblazer surveillance program, asserted the NSA 4+1, violated the Fourth Amendment of the US Constitution by collecting Americans' telephone, email, and Internet communications without first obtaining a warrant from a federal judge. Binney told me, "Yeah, I have a problem with that. It's criminal. It's unconstitutional. . . . That's why I left there as fast as I could, because I couldn't be a party to it." Binney said that his ThinThread program would have avoided this problem, for he had inserted a feature that "scrubbed" the identities of US citizens whose communications were intercepted, thus protecting their privacy (though the NSA could still learn their identities if it convinced a judge to issue a warrant to reveal them).

"We were concerned about these constitutional issues even before we investigated their [NSA 4+1's] complaint," Crane said of his team. "We had received other whistleblower filings that flagged the issue, notably concerning the 'Terrorism Information Awareness Program,' which had drawn expressions of concern from Congress as well."

Buoyed by Crane's office ruling, the NSA 4+1's whistle-blowing initially appeared to have succeeded: it emboldened Congress to kill Trailblazer.

Congress had dramatically increased military and intelligence spending in the wake of the 9/11 terror attacks, but it had also put NSA on notice: the agency's notoriously poor acquisition and bookkeeping practices had to improve or else. After the Senate Armed Services Committee concluded that "insufficient progress" had been made, Congress in 2003 took an extraordinary step: in effect, it took away NSA's credit card, transferring its spending authority for multimillion dollar programs to the Under Secretary of Defense.

When Crane's office endorsed the NSA 4+1's accusations a year later, it was the last straw. Even members of Congress who traditionally shoveled money at the military industrial complex with few questions asked had grown troubled by

Trailblazer's continuing cost overruns. Hayden was summoned to Capitol Hill, where he had to admit that Trailblazer was "several hundreds of millions of dollars" over budget and years behind schedule. In 2006, Congress shut down the program.

For the NSA 4+1 and Crane, however, this apparent victory was only the beginning of a dark, twisting saga that would change their lives forever. And because warrantless surveillance continued through other means after Trailblazer was killed, this saga eventually called onto history's stage a young NSA contractor by the name of Edward Snowden.

Smelling a Rat in the IG's Office

To John Crane, the most striking finding in his staff's report on the NSA 4+1 didn't concern constitutional abuses or multibillion dollar cost overruns. Rather, it was that more than one of the whistle-blowers had repeatedly expressed fear that they would face retaliation for speaking out. Federal law expressly protected against retaliation by guaranteeing a whistle-blower's anonymity. Crane soon found himself fighting for this cornerstone principle of the whistle-blower law in the face of repeated demands from his superiors to violate it.

The fact that the NSA 4+1 report highlighted a fear of reprisal was "absolutely extraordinary," said Crane. It told him that the investigators in the case "were making a point"—and that the whistle-blowers' fears must have been exceptionally well-founded.

This made further investigation imperative, Crane told me, but he was overruled, he claimed, by Henry Shelley, the IG's deputy general counsel. According to Crane, Shelley's refusal was motivated partly by an alleged antipathy to the man who would have done the investigation: Dan Meyer, the director of the IG's Civilian Reprisal Investigations unit. Meyer, a former Navy officer, was openly gay, which Shelley, an officer in the Naval Reserve, allegedly found repugnant.

In addition, Meyer had been a whistle-blower after surviving an explosion on the USS *Iowa* in 1989 that killed forty-seven crewmen. When the Navy's investigation appeared to blame the explosion on a secret homosexual love affair gone wrong, Meyer was one of the eyewitnesses who questioned the conclusion; a second Navy investigation withdrew the accusation. Shelley allegedly told Crane that he regarded Meyer's whistle-blowing as an attack on the Navy as an institution and a personal insult to Shelley as a Naval Reserve officer.

As noted above, Shelley declined to be interviewed for this book. So did Lynne Halbrooks, who allegedly joined with Shelley and clashed with Crane in her roles as the Pentagon's deputy inspector general and acting inspector general. Therefore the account that follows largely reflects the recollections of Crane, buttressed by the documentary record and my additional interviews with other individuals. I have done my utmost to verify its accuracy and heed Shelley's request to be "fair to all involved."

"For Shelley to refuse to investigate [the NSA whistle-blowers' fears of retaliation] goes against IG rules and regulations and you can argue that it goes against statute," said Crane. "You would think that's exactly the thing we want to investigate—people are concerned about being investigated because they're talking to us!

As deputy general counsel, Henry Shelley outranked Crane and wielded decisive power over what the IG's office did and did not do. "He was the attorney in charge of all whistleblower reprisal cases," said Crane, "so he could stop any case he wanted. . . . No reprisal case could be undertaken or findings issued without Henry Shelley signing off on it."

Crane lost that battle, and a bigger clash lay ahead. After the *New York Times* finally published James Risen and Eric Lichtblau's landmark article on the Bush-Cheney administration's domestic surveillance, the White House was apoplectic—and determined to find who leaked the information to the *Times*.

"I actually told President Bush after the story went out that based upon the inaccuracies in Lichtblau's stories I suspected that what they were getting was water cooler talk," Hayden told me. "And most of the water coolers were in the Department of Justice."

What did President Bush say in reply?

"He just shook his head," Hayden said.

Inside the Pentagon's IG office, Shelley allegedly had a different suspicion. Crane said that during a meeting in the IG's office, Shelley urged telling the Justice Department about the NSA 4+1; after all, their whistle-blower complaint had objected to the very kind of surveillance practices described in the *Times*. Crane objected strenuously, arguing that informing anyone, much less Justice Department investigators, of a whistle-blower's name would violate the law's guarantee of anonymity for whistle-blowers.

After the formal meeting ended, Shelley and Crane continued their disagreement in the hallway outside the IG's office, Crane recalled. "I reached into my breast pocket and pulled out my copy of the Inspector General Act," he said. "I had to carry it around with me because Henry and I argued so much. I was concerned that he was violating the law. Our voices weren't raised, but the conversation was, I would say, very intense and agitated. Henry said that he was the general counsel and the general counsel was in charge of handling things with the Justice Department and he would do things his way."

There the disagreement between Crane and Shelley stalled. Or so it seemed until eighteen months later, when on the morning of July 26, 2007, FBI agents with guns drawn rushed across the yards of Binney, Wiebe, Loomis, and Roark, pounded on their front doors and demanded entry. Binney was toweling off after a shower when agents accosted him in his bathroom; he and his wife suddenly found themselves with guns aimed directly between their eyes, the retired NSA man recalled.

Smelling a rat, Crane challenged Shelley: had he or someone else in the IG's office furnished the names of the NSA whistle-blowers to the FBI? The report by Crane's staff had been highly classified; the version later made public had roughly 90 percent of its contents redacted. Very few people could have known the whistle-blowers' names, and most of those people would have been inside the IG's office.

Shelley refused to discuss the matter, according to Crane.

The battle escalated. Four months later, it was Drake whose house endured an early morning raid by federal agents as his family looked on in shock. Prosecutors threatened him with life in prison, then offered a plea deal—a shorter sentence if he confessed his crimes—and later a second deal as well. Drake responded, "I refuse to bargain with the truth."

In 2009, Justice Department officials—who now answered to a new president and attorney general, Barack Obama and Eric Holder, respectively—threatened Drake's fellow whistle-blowers with prison terms. As detailed in Risen's 2014 book, *Pay Any Price: Greed, Power and Endless War*, agents demanded of Roark that she plead guilty to perjury, a felony, for allegedly lying to them about who had leaked information to the *New York Times* and *Baltimore Sun*; they also demanded that she implicate Drake in illegal behavior. She refused.

Binney decided to fire back—and have fun doing it—after the Justice Department told his lawyer it was preparing to file charges. "I called Tom Drake, knowing that the FBI was tapping his phone, and told him to make sure his lawyer knew that I had evidence that would allow us to charge the government with malicious prosecution," Binney told me.

Just before their houses were raided in 2007, Binney explained, he, Wiebe, Loomis, and Roark met to discuss a business venture. The algorithms and other technical tools that had been developed for the Thin Thread program could also be employed to detect waste, fraud, and abuse within the Medicare system, they believed. Since the NSA didn't want to deploy Thin Thread, why not use it to save taxpayers money elsewhere while profiting themselves? The malicious prosecution angle arose because the group had invited two other people to the business meeting, but neither was raided or threatened with indictment. "I was pulling the FBI's chain to get my message to the Justice Department," Binney said. "Well, what do you know, one month after my phone conversation with Drake, we all received letters of immunity." (Except Drake, of course, who had not attended the business meeting.)

Crane now tussled again with his superiors. After Drake was indicted, his lawyers at GAP filed a Freedom of Information Act request, seeking all documents related to the Pentagon IG's investigation of the NSA 4+1's whistle-blowing complaint. Part of Crane's job was to process Freedom of Information Act (FOIA) requests. In this instance, he was ordered not to release any FOIA documents until *after* Drake's trial. The order, which obstructed Drake's pursuit of justice, came from both Shelley and from Halbrooks, who had been named principle deputy inspector general eight months earlier, Crane told me. Crane strongly disagreed but lost this skirmish as well.

A new battle opened when Crane received a letter concerning "one of the most potentially explosive matters I had encountered in my career at the Department of Defense's Office of the Inspector General." In December 2010, GAP went on the offensive, filing a legal complaint that Drake was being retaliated against because of his participation in the NSA 4+1's whistle-blower action. Many of the crimes alleged against Drake were "based in part, or entirely, on information that Mr. Drake provided to the [Department of Defense] IG" during its investigation of the NSA 4+1's complaint, GAP's letter pointed out.

Crane was at once alarmed and revolted. GAP's complaint seemed to confirm his suspicion that someone in the IG's office had fingered Drake to Justice Department investigators. Worse, the unmistakable correspondence between Drake's indictment and his testimony to Crane's staff suggested that Drake's entire testimony, not just his name, had been shared—an utter violation of law. The Whistleblower Protection Act says the government must protect a whistle-blower's identity unless disclosing the identity is, quote, "'unavoidable,'" Devine explained. "Our suspicion is that this disclosure was deliberate."

Drake's retaliation complaint demanded investigation, Crane told Halbrooks. Joined by Shelley, Halbrooks rejected Crane's demand, according to Crane, adding that he wasn't being a "good team player" and if he didn't shape up, she would make life difficult for him.

Lying to a Judge Is of Course a Crime

Then came an astonishing wrinkle that put the entire IG office in legal hazard. Drake's trial was drawing near; by law his retaliation complaint had to be answered in some fashion. But that was going to be tricky because, as Shelley informed Crane, the relevant documents had been destroyed. Lower level staff "had fucked up," Crane said Shelley told him: they had shredded the documents in a routine purge of the IG's vast stores of confidential material.

Crane literally could not believe his ears, he recalled. "I told Henry that destruction of documents under such circumstances was, as he knew, a very serious matter and could lead to the inspector general being accused of obstructing a criminal investigation." Shelley replied, according to Crane, that it didn't have to be a problem if everyone was a good team player.

On February 15, 2011, Shelley and Halbrooks sent the judge in the Drake case a letter that repeated the excuse Crane had been given: the requested documents had been destroyed, by mistake, during a routine purge. This routine purge, the letter assured Judge Richard D. Bennett, took place *before* Drake was indicted.

"Lynne and Henry had frozen me out by then, so I had no input into their letter to Judge Bennett," Crane said. Crane would later allege in his own whistle-blower complaint that Halbrooks and Shelley had lied to the judge in Drake's case. Crane told me, "Lying to a judge in a criminal case is of course a crime."

"It's a felony to lie to a judge in that situation," clarified Devine, citing 18 US Code 1001, known among the legal fraternity as the "False Statement Statute." Asked how an experienced, high-level attorney such as Henry Shelley might have dared commit such a transgression, Devine smiled and said, "People who know better can be blinded by their own arrogance. That's how people get caught—they get sloppy."

In the end, the government's case against Drake collapsed, though not because of Shelley and Halbrook's alleged obstruction of justice, which at the time was unknown. Rather, other skulduggery was afoot. For example, one count of the indictment alleged that Drake illegally removed classified documents from his office and took them home. But the documents were not classified at the time Drake took them home, so prosecutors apparently leaned on officials at the NSA to *classify them retroactively.* Judges tend to frown on that kind of thing.

Prosecutors eventually offered Drake a third, much less onerous plea deal: all criminal charges would be dropped if Drake pleaded guilty to a misdemeanor for improperly storing government documents on his home computer. He accepted the deal.

When it came time for Judge Bennett to announce a sentence, he condemned the government in no uncertain terms. The judge found it "extraordinary" that the government had barged into Drake's home, indicted him, but then dropped the case on the eve of trial as if it wasn't a big deal after all. No American, he added, should have to wait "two and a half years after their home is searched to find out if they're going to be indicted or not. I find that unconscionable. Unconscionable. It is at the very root of what this country was founded on, against general warrants of the British. It was one of the most fundamental things in the Bill of Rights, that this country was not to be exposed to people knocking on the door with government authority and coming into their homes."

"Unclean! Unclean!"

"We are now becoming a police state," Diane Roark told the TV news program *Frontline* in 2014. Referring to the "huge database" of individuals' communications the NSA was accumulating, Roark warned that this personal information "is not only going to be used for criminal prosecution, it's going to be used against political enemies. And we are the canaries, the five of us [the NSA 4 +1]. We are the canaries in the coalmine. We never did anything wrong. All we did was oppose this program. And for that, they just ran over us.

"To be under investigation for six or seven years," Roark added, was "a massive stress. But it will have all been worth it if the US public gets away from this view, 'I don't have anything to hide.' I cannot understand how people can say such a thing. . . . If you have any political beliefs at all, it can be used against you by the opposition if they're in power."

"They're saying, 'We're doing this to protect you,'" Binney told me. "I will tell you that that's exactly what the Nazis said in Special Order 48 in 1933—we're doing this to protect you. And that's how they got rid of all of their political opponents." Special Order 48 existed before Hitler seized power, but it was he who used the law most ruthlessly. After the Reichstag (the German parliament) was set ablaze in 1933, Hitler, who had been named chancellor as part of a power sharing agreement in parliament, said that the fire was the start of a communist revolution. He pressured the German president to invoke Special Order 48, which suspended rights of assembly, habeas corpus, freedom of the press, and other civil liberties. The Nazis then arrested and otherwise neutralized communists and other political opponents. Invoking Special Order 48 enabled Hitler to claim he was acting legally even as he established a brutal dictatorship. The lesson here: those seeking authoritarian powers often invent or exaggerate specters of terror to stampede the public into accepting a suspension of civil liberties.

"Do you know that the Russians are now copying what we're doing, under their SORM program?" Binney asked. "NSA learned these techniques from one totalitarian system [East Germany's Stasi], now the Russians are adopting it from us. Totalitarian states are mimicking us, isn't that great?" he said, sarcasm dripping from his lips.

Comparing US government practices to those of totalitarians and Nazis, warning about an emergent "police state"—these are strong statements, so it's worth remembering who was making them. Binney, Roark, and the other NSA 4+1 whistle-blowers were not a bunch of left-wing peace nuts. They spent their professional lives inside the US intelligence apparatus—devoted, they thought, to protection of the homeland and defense of the Constitution. They were self-described political conservatives, highly educated, respectful of evidence, careful with words. And they were saying, on the basis of personal experience, that the United States government had been taken over by criminals who bent the government's awesome powers to their own nefarious purposes. They were saying that laws, regulations, and technologies had been put in place, in secret, that threatened to overturn the democratic governance Americans took for granted and shrink their liberties to a vanishing point. And they were saying that something needed to be done about all this before it was too late.

Binney singled out former Vice President Dick Cheney as the main driving force toward what Binney called "totalitarianism" in America. At NSA, Binney told me, the Stellar Wind mass surveillance program "was called a Cheney blood oath." The few officials who were "read into" (i.e., cleared to know about) the program's existence knew that it came from the vice president's office and there would be hell to pay if they breathed a word. "It's like in old westerns," Binney explained, "when the cowboy and the Indian cut their palms, put their blood together and then they were blood brothers forever."

Cheney's blood oath was a more extreme version of the cult of secrecy that had long permeated US military and intelligence circles. John Crane saw the mindset in action the first few times he entered zones of the Pentagon where top secret intelligence operations were under way. Crane himself had all the top clearances necessary, as well as the code words required to open doors and the like. Nevertheless, he was treated like a leper.

"I was walking around the building, I had my [security] badge on," he recalled. "Suddenly, the intelligence guys who didn't recognize me would stand up in their cubicles and shout, 'Unclean! Unclean!' And everyone else in the room immediately shut their laptops and refused to talk to me. That's the cult of intelligence: if you're not part of the cult, you shouldn't be there. The first couple of times it happened to me, I was so shocked. I learned that I needed to have my 'No Escort Required' badge prominently displayed or there would be misunderstandings."

Daniel Ellsberg saw a similar mindset during his years as a high-level Pentagon and White House adviser; it left him convinced that too much secrecy is bad not only for democracy but also for the ability of the president and his top advisers to make well-informed policy. In his memoir, Ellsberg argued that the debacle of Vietnam demonstrated "how the system of secrecy and lying could give [a president] options he would be better off without." Excessive secrecy made it "harder for the president to resist pressures from the military. Secrecy from the public [also] averted countervailing pressures from that direction."

Ellsberg tried to warn Henry Kissinger, when the two men were still on friendly terms, about the siren-like seductions of secrecy. In late 1968, after Nixon had been elected and announced that Kissinger would be his national security adviser, Ellsberg met with Kissinger and alerted him to a challenge that Ellsberg said he wished someone had warned him about beforehand: the dizzying effect of receiving "a whole slew of special clearances . . . that are higher than top secret." First, Ellsberg told Kissinger, "you'll be exhilarated by some of this new information [you will learn via the clearances]." This feeling, Ellsberg continued, "will last for about two weeks." But soon, he added, as you get used to having all this new information, "you will forget there ever was a time when you didn't have it, and you'll be aware only of the fact that you have it now and most others don't and that all those *other* people are fools. . . . [As a result, it will] become very hard for you to *learn* from anybody who doesn't have these clearances."

"Cheney grew up under Nixon," Binney observed, referring to Cheney's beginning as a low-level staffer in Nixon's White House. "He wanted to have the same kind of insight to his political enemies Nixon got with Nixon's secret surveillance programs: COINTELPRO was the FBI's program, CHAOS was the CIA's and Minaret was NSA's. Minaret actually spied on Frank Church (the Democratic senator from Idaho who led the congressional investigations in the 1970s that led to restrictions on US intelligence operations). Cheney detested those restrictions, by the way. I estimate that Nixon was only able to spy on a few thousand people. Today, because technology has advanced, the same three agencies are spying on roughly 270 million Americans—that's the number of people using cell phones, landlines, fixed or mobile computers and credit cards."

Although championed and vastly expanded by Cheney, the spying continued under Obama. Some restrictions were added, but they were modest enough that Michael Hayden greeted them with boyish relief. The USA FREEDOM Act Obama signed in 2014 contained two reforms. The first stipulated that the government no longer hold the records of all the phone calls made in the United States; instead, this metadata will be held by the telecommunications companies themselves. (At the Bush-Cheney administration's insistence, the companies previously had allowed the NSA to tap directly into their data centers.) The second required the NSA to obtain an individual warrant before accessing these records—a return to the status quo pre-Bush-Cheney. "And this is it, after two years?" Hayden exclaimed. "Cool!"

Keep in mind that it was Obama's continuation of the Bush-Cheney surveillance that convinced Snowden to blow the whistle in the first place. Snowden did not vote for Obama in 2008—he was a fan of Ron Paul, the libertarian congressman whose son, Senator Rand Paul, pursued the Republican 2016 presidential nomination. But Snowden took note of candidate Obama's pledges to reform surveillance policy and decided to see if a *President* Obama would do as promised. When Snowden saw no real improvement—when he instead saw Obama's Justice Department raid and arrest the NSA 4+1 and persecute Drake in particular—he concluded that he'd been wrong to give Barack Obama the benefit of the doubt. Now, it was time to act.

"[President Obama] could end mass surveillance tomorrow with a stroke of his pen," Snowden later said, referring to Obama's authority to sign an executive order. "If the president of all people is not willing to stand up for our rights, what kind of message does that send to citizens, to children and people around the world about what our values really mean to our government?"

Double Standards Are Standard

"I don't call Snowden a hero, but he did an extremely important public service," Binney said. "He probably should be indicted for stealing government property, but not under the Espionage Act. The law should be applied equally, though—which means that we should also be trying President Bush, Cheney, Hayden and everyone else who was running these programs. And then try the [equivalent] officials in the Obama administration. If you don't want to do the rest of them first, then don't do Snowden."

Double standards had been a second motivation for Snowden. No one moment pushed him over the line, he later recalled; it was rather an accumulation of outrages. One particular outrage he cited was watching James Clapper, the director of National Intelligence, tell an absolute lie when testifying to the US Senate about the Presidential Surveillance Program on March 12, 2013. Democrat Ron Wyden of Oregon, who as a member of the Intelligence Committee had learned the outlines of the program, asked Clapper if the government was collecting "any type of data at all on millions or hundreds of millions of Americans." Clapper replied, "No, sir. Not wittingly." Clapper told this lie deliberately and with forethought: the day before, Wyden's staff had sent him the list of questions he would be asked.

Lying to Congress was a crime, but Clapper was not charged; his sole punishment was public embarrassment after Snowden's leak revealed his lie. "Baldly lying to the public without repercussion is evidence of a subverted democracy,"

Snowden said. "The consent of the governed is not consent if it is not informed."

Double standards appeared to be standard for national security crimes: one set of rules and punishments for the big boys, a different set for underlings. Four months before Clapper lied to Congress, the CIA director, General David Petraeus, resigned because of an affair with his biographer, Paula Broadwell. Later, a deeper reason emerged for his resignation: FBI investigators had discovered that Petraeus shared highly classified information—code names for intelligence programs, war plans, names of undercover operatives—with Broadwell. When confronted, Petraeus denied the accusations.

It was a crime to lie during a federal investigation, which may explain why FBI agents later took the unusual step of telling reporters they were not happy when Petraeus was given what they regarded as too light of a sentence. Under a plea deal, Petraeus pled guilty to a misdemeanor: unauthorized removal and retention of classified information. He received no jail time, only two years' probation and a $100,000 fine. He apparently did not lose his security clearances, thus enabling him to continue serving on corporate boards and commanding six-figure honoraria for speaking gigs, a handful of which would recover his legal costs.

Compare that outcome with the ruin visited upon Thomas Drake, who did not reveal an iota of classified information. And consider that most recent national security whistle-blowers have been treated much more like Drake than like Petraeus.

Take John Kiriakou. This former CIA agent had the distinction of being the only US official jailed as a result of the torture program that US forces operated in the post-9/11 era. Countless officials, up to and including President Bush and

Vice President Cheney, knew about, approved or carried out torture during the so-called war on terrorism. Torture is a crime under the Geneva Convention, which makes it a crime under the laws of the United States, a signatory to that convention. Yet no US official was charged, much less convicted, for these crimes. This was another case where Barack Obama said one thing as a candidate but did another as president. Candidate Obama was an outspoken critic of torture; once elected, he declined to bring charges, explaining that it was important for the country to "look forward, not backwards."

Kiriakou appeared to have been jailed not because he committed torture, but because he told the public about it. As a CIA field officer, he had participated in the capture of Abu Zubaydah, allegedly a top aide of Osama bin Laden. In a 2007 interview with ABC News, Kiriakou said that the CIA had used a torture technique known as a "waterboarding" on Zubaydah. The revelation sparked considerable public discussion, with Bush officials insisting that waterboarding— in which a victim is tied down and water poured down his throat until he begins drowning—did not constitute torture.

In January 2012, Kiriakou was charged with disclosing classified information to journalists. Like Drake before and Snowden after him, he was represented by Jesselyn Radack, who bargained the charges down. In the end, Kiriakou pled guilty to a single count and was sentenced to thirty months in prison, plus another three months under house arrest. Petraeus—who by this time had resigned but had not yet been accused of handing classified information to his mistress—praised the verdict as "an important victory for our agency . . . [that demonstrated there are] consequences for those who believe they are above the laws."

Hayden, on the other hand, expressed a more beneficent view of Kiriakou, as he had of Drake. Declaring himself "glad that the FBI case [against Drake] collapsed of its own weight," Hayden told me that "I feel the same thing about John Kiriakou, who I don't think should have spent two and a half years in jail for what he did. I'd have stripped him of his clearance, and Kiriakou is an idiot, but I would not have put him in jail. That's a pretty heavy sanction on a guy with a young family. You know, I'm just a soft-hearted guy," said the man who repeatedly defended use of the torture that Kiriakou exposed.

For his part, Kiriakou insisted that he was punished for blowing the whistle. "I have maintained from the day of my arrest that my case was never about leaking," he told the *New York Times* after his release in February 2015 following nearly two years in prison. "My case was about torture. The CIA never forgave me for talking about torture."

Three months after Kiriakou's release, another former CIA officer, Jeffrey Sterling, was sent to jail after blowing the whistle on a separate case of CIA conduct. Like many whistle-blowers, Sterling began as a true believer. On his first day of work at the CIA, he did not proceed directly from the parking lot into the rear of the building as everyone else did; he walked around to the front entrance so he could first gaze upon the agency's official seal emblazoned with the words Central Intelligence Agency of the United States. "That's how much working at the CIA meant to him," said Norman Solomon, a journalist and activist who championed Sterling's case.

Sterling was convicted of passing classified information to the reporter James Risen—not for the *New York Times* story Risen did (with Eric Lichtblau) about the Bush-Cheney administration's surveillance program, but for a chapter in his book, *State of War*. The chapter described a CIA program that involved passing phony nuclear weapons designs to the government of Iran in hopes of derailing Iran's alleged pursuit of nuclear weapons capability.

Sterling emphatically denied having leaked information, but freely admitted he had alerted the Senate Intelligence Committee to the grave dangers he felt the Iran program presented—to wit, that it would help, not hinder, an adversary of the United States to acquire nuclear weapons. Like the NSA 4+1 whistle-blowers before him, Sterling went through official channels to blow the whistle on what he considered "a specific and substantial" threat to public safety.

But prosecutors had the president's surveillance program at their disposal, and they used it to present circumstantial evidence that Sterling had passed information to Risen. Metadata showed that Sterling and Risen had indeed exchanged phone calls and emails. The metadata did not, however, disclose what they talked about; it could have been the Iran program, it could have been something else entirely. Nevertheless, prosecutors put Sterling's whistle-blowing to Congress together with the metadata to argue that he was Risen's source.

It did not help that Sterling, one of the CIA's very few African American case officers, had previously accused the agency of racial bias. Sterling sued the CIA in August 2001, alleging that he had been passed over for assignments that led to promotions; it was the first such lawsuit in the agency's history. A month later, the 9/11 terrorist attacks left Sterling so eager to fight back that he instructed his lawyer to offer to withdraw the suit so he could return to work. Instead the agency fired him, with CIA deputy executive director John Brennan delivering the news to Sterling personally. A court later threw out the lawsuit, explaining that a trial would jeopardize "state secrets."

"The moment that they felt there was a leak, every finger pointed to Jeffrey Sterling," Sterling said in a documentary about his case, *The Invisible Man*. Although his lawsuit had been dismissed years earlier, prosecutors cited it to buttress their contention that he was a "selfish and vindictive" individual who sought to take revenge against the CIA by leaking to Risen. The *New York Times* reporter and author, in keeping with journalistic practice, refused to name his sources, asserting that he would go to jail himself before doing so. For Risen's colleagues in the media, that became the preeminent issue: whether a reporter would face repercussions for doing his job. When it became clear that Risen would not be prosecuted, media interest in the proceedings waned. The jury, which included no African Americans, found Sterling guilty of nine felony counts.

Jeffrey Sterling was sentenced to forty-two months in prison in May 2015, five weeks after Petraeus received no jail time for passing classified information to his mistress. Sterling's attorney, Radack, blasted the double standard, telling the *Democracy Now* broadcast news program, "The top three past CIA directors, including Leon Panetta, including General David Petraeus, including [John] Brennan, have all leaked covert identities and suffered no consequence for it."

"Surreal" was the word Sterling and his wife, Holly, repeatedly used to describe this whole experience: first, the accusations against him; then a trial that found him guilty on only circumstantial evidence; and finally the judge's sentencing that dispatched him to the federal corrections institution in Littleton, Colorado, on June 16, 2015. With help from Norman Solomon and his organization, the Institute for Public Accuracy, Holly Sterling in October 2015 became the first spouse of a jailed CIA agent to speak out publicly; at a news conference in the National Press Building in Washington, she appealed to President Obama to pardon her husband, who she insisted had "done nothing wrong."

Barring such a presidential pardon or other unexpected intervention, Jeffrey Sterling, once a true believer in the CIA and the American way, will remain in prison until December 2018.

The Goal Is to Demoralize the Whistle-blower

Meanwhile, the fate of John Crane hung in the balance in more ways than one. On a practical level, there was the future of his job; on a philosophical level, there was the question of whether his faith in the goodness and reliability of the system would be validated.

As for his job, Crane's bosses at last forced him out. Crane claimed he was a victim of what he called "perjured testimony" by both Shelley and Halbrooks, and that Halbrooks was motivated by her alleged desire to be promoted from acting Inspector General to official Inspector General. What's more, in an Alice In Wonderland twist, Shelley and Halbrooks, according to Crane, then ruled on their own perjured testimony—making them simultaneously the prosecution, witnesses, and judges in the case.

Halbrooks put Crane on administrative leave in February 2013, four months before Edward Snowden's revelations rocked the world and suddenly made whistle-blowing a topic of daily conversation for millions. "Administrative leave" was US government-speak for "forced resignation." Crane was forbidden to come to the office, and his pay and security clearances were suspended. He was not, however, fired. It was not easy to fire a federal worker in the absence of compelling evidence of incompetence, insubordination, or wrongdoing; federal workers had due process rights most private sector workers lacked. This may explain why some federal whistle-blowers who got retaliated against didn't lose their jobs outright; they were punished in pettier ways.

Bogdan Dzakovic, the Federal Aviation Administration official whose darkly comic exploits testing airport security I wrote about in *Vanity Fair*, was never fired, for instance, despite his bosses' undisguised antipathy toward him. Instead they put him on the midnight shift at Washington's Dulles International Airport, where the only thing that relieved his boredom was the occasional telephone call from an individual claiming to be a space alien. The goal of such management tactics, said Devine, was to demoralize the whistle-blower so he or she will quit on their own. Crane said that he got similar treatment: "Lynne said that she could make it so uncomfortable for me that I would want to leave."

Is it any surprise that the grandson of the man who faced down Hitler at gunpoint did not surrender to such attacks? That he instead stood his ground and fought back? That he took his adversaries to court and actually expected to be vindicated?

Almost as if reenacting his grandfather's showdown with Hitler on the night of the Munich Beer Hall Putsch, Crane in effect told Lynne Halbrooks and Henry Shelley that *In this way you will never conquer me.* He walked out of the Pentagon and before long made his way to the Government Accountability Project. "I approached GAP because Tom Devine had an outstanding reputation as a whistleblower lawyer and advocate," recalled Crane, who had first met Devine and other GAP attorneys while running the Pentagon's whistle-blower unit. Crane had even brokered a meeting between GAP and Halbrooks to try to improve the two camps' relationship in the wake of the Drake indictment.

GAP welcomed Crane with open arms, not least because his inside knowledge gave them valuable inside knowledge for the fight to defend Drake. Crane's affidavits detailing how Halbrooks and Shelley allegedly violated legal standards in dealing with Drake's whistle-blowing enabled Devine to file a blistering response to the IG's report. Since Halbrooks and Shelley had allegedly been the chief tormentors of Drake—first by identifying him to Justice Department investigators, later by obstructing justice in his court trial—they had a conflict of interest that obviously disqualified them from "any involvement . . . [in] the whistleblower reprisal investigation of Mr. Drake," Devine wrote.

Crane's case also had an intrinsic appeal to the whistleblower advocates at GAP. Crane was not just any whistleblower: he had run the whistle-blowing unit of the biggest agency in the US government, the Department of Defense. "I was in charge of the DoD hotline for 1.3 million [military] service members and 700,000 civilians, almost two million federal employees in all," Crane recalled. For such an official to share secrets from the belly of the beast was a treat for Devine, who said, "The more John told me about his experiences trying to fight the good fight at DoD, the more I wanted to work with him."

At another level, however, Devine and Clark did not know quite what to make of Crane. Here was a guy who gave every appearance of genuinely believing that whistle-blowers inside the national security apparatus could and should get fair and confidential treatment. Clark and Devine had seen too many examples of the opposite over the years to harbor any such sentiments. They were not jaded; they still fought hard for their clients, but they tended to presume the worst about how a bureaucracy would operate. Their presumptions hardened during the Bush-Cheney years, when aggressive White House rhetoric—"Either you are with us, or you are with the terrorists," Bush declared days after 9/11—helped create a climate of fear and intimidation throughout the country, especially in Washington. The presidency of Obama, who repudiated his campaign promises about transparency and protecting whistle-blowers in favor of a harsher crackdown on open government, fortified their convictions.

But Crane, it seemed, never got the memo about the war with terrorism overturning constitutional government in the home of the brave. He still believed that the system was fundamentally sound. Clark and Devine admired his faith in the system even as it baffled them. "John's the real deal," said Devine. "I don't know how he survived all those years inside the Pentagon thinking the way he does, but it's not a pose. He really believes it."

The Third Man Fights Back

Crane's counteroffensive began February 9, 2015, when GAP filed a whistle-blower disclosure accusing Halbrooks and Shelley of improper conduct. Accompanying the disclosure were three affidavits from Crane—hundreds of pages detailing the episodes described in this book and much else. Summarizing the case, Devine said, "John Crane's story demonstrates that anyone whose job is to protect whistle-blowers has a very dangerous job."

Astonishingly, it was a job that Crane wanted back. In his mind, the top goal of his legal action was to be reinstated in his old post as the Pentagon's assistant inspector general in charge of whistle-blowing.

Devine thought Crane was crazy, or at least naive. "I'm not sure I've ever worked with a whistleblower who was more of a Boy Scout than John is," Devine said. "It's what makes John the kind of person he is and the kind of whistleblower he is. He truly believes in playing it straight and that the system will work as advertised. As his lawyer, I have to respect that, even as I warn him that the system may just be stringing him along."

Crane smiled calmly when hearing all the reasons why his return as the Pentagon's chief whistle-blower official seems far-fetched. His bosses hated him—why would they ever allow him back? And even if a legal ruling ordered his reinstatement, why would he want to go back to work for people who had shown themselves eager to make his life miserable?

"I want to give the system every opportunity to work the way it should," said Crane, seated in a conference room at GAP in the same coat and tie attire expected at the Pentagon. "Tom and I have enough skills so the system should be able to respond. I am in effect testing the system. I believe that the system, if it works properly, will work to my benefit."

To Crane, it was a simple matter of right and wrong. It was not he who had broken the law, it was Halbrooks and Shelley; therefore, it was they, not he, who should pay the price. Until his run-ins with them, Crane told me, "I had worked for ten separate agency heads at DOD and never been asked to do something I thought was illegal. I had never been exposed to an individual who was willing to use their office for personal gain. I was shocked."

But still, I pressed, why go back to working for individuals who despise you? Is that really how you want to spend your life?

"Well, Lynne is no longer there," Crane replied. After she wasn't promoted to inspector general, Halbrooks left government. In May 2015 she was named a partner at Holland & Knight, a law firm with offices throughout the United States that represented corporate clients, including military contractors. "She's now representing the companies it was our mandate [at the Pentagon's IG office] to investigate," Crane added.

"But doesn't that still leave Shelley?" I asked. "You clashed with him just as much, and as general counsel couldn't he thwart you at every turn if you came back?"

"If he's still there," Crane replied, eyes twinkling.

A second aim of Crane's legal action, it seems, was to put enough heat on Shelley to push him out as general counsel. If Crane's whistle-blower disclosure was validated, it would have the practical effect of putting Shelley under investigation. Federal investigators would begin looking into Crane's allegations, reading his affidavits, reviewing documents and interviewing witnesses, including Shelley himself. Perhaps investigators would find that Shelley had perfectly legal explanations for his actions. Perhaps they would conclude that Crane was making everything up—striking back at Shelley in return for getting rid of him.

But the fact of Shelley being investigated would put him, and the Pentagon Inspector General's office, under a cloud and perhaps lead the secretary of defense or members of Congress to conclude that it was time for fresh blood. "For a general counsel to be under investigation calls into question his activities throughout the time he was general counsel, and that can be used as reason to have him removed," said Crane. "Nobody wants a general counsel who's under investigation. It looks terrible."

Only an independent investigation could determine where the truth lay, and there Crane's legal action faced a critical hurdle. GAP had filed his whistle-blower disclosure with the Office of Special Counsel, which would investigate whether Crane had been punished because he properly carried out his professional duties. The OSC is a government-wide agency that adjudicates whistle-blower cases that bubble up throughout the federal bureaucracy, generally cases that individual agencies cannot resolve on their own.

If the OSC ruled in Crane's favor, it would start a clock running: the secretary of defense would have sixty days to report back to the OSC and establish a joint plan to undertake a more detailed investigation of Crane's allegations. "We're optimistic the OSC will find in John's favor and his charges will get a real hearing," said Devine. "That's always the toughest thing for a whistleblower, to get a real hearing. The OSC asked us to specify precisely which laws we believe were broken." Grinning, the lawyer added, "Our amended filing had a whole separate Appendix with all the violations."

The Office of Special Counsel ruled in Crane's favor in March 2016, declaring in a letter to Secretary of Defense Ashton Carter that there was a "substantial likelihood" Crane's charges about Halbrooks and Shelley's handling of the Thomas Drake case were true. The "substantial likelihood" finding was considerably stronger than an alternative decision the OSC could have made. Had the OSC concluded that there was merely a "reasonable belief" Crane was right, the Secretary of Defense would have been notified but not required to take any action. Instead, Secretary Carter was now legally obligated to begin a second, more comprehensive investigation of the case within sixty days. Since the Pentagon's Inspector General Office could not credibly investigate itself, this second investigation would be undertaken by the Department of Justice. Said Devine, "We are very much looking forward to assisting in this new investigation and securing justice both for Drake and Crane."

"This Is Something I Have to Do"

Crane's was "a long and twisting story," as he himself described it, and he was still far from victory. If the stories recounted in this book show anything, it is that logic and the law are easily sidelined when government officials confront whistle-blowers who bear unwelcome tidings. Especially in the national security area, double standards are standard, power plays naked, lying ubiquitous. Is it cynical to imagine that even the new Justice Department investigation GAP and Crane had secured would reject or at least deflect Crane's allegations, making a mockery of his desire to get his old job back?

Such a result would have to shake Crane's faith that in the end the system works properly, would it not? As a practical matter, he could still file a whistle-blower retaliation complaint, and Devine said Crane would do so. Nevertheless, the military justice system would have failed him. Growing up in a military family, he had been taught that one must do the right thing and trust that justice would win out. Crane had gone on to stake his professional career on this faith, to the point that he ended up being driven out of a well-paying, rewarding job he loved. Would all this now be repudiated?

Crane and Devine respected each other professionally and seemed to have a personal fondness as well, but philosophically they held sharply different views on the nature of the beast confronting them. Crane saw the problem of official wrongdoing primarily as a function of individual virtue or vice. Asked what lessons the American people should draw from his experiences, he replied, "Congress writes and passes the laws of the land, but they are implemented by human beings. And you have to be careful about the human beings you put in charge, because they can subvert all the best intentions of the Congress and the executive branch."

Devine saw the problem as systemic, rooted in power relations and the clash of institutional interests. "Whether it is a government agency or a private corporation, institutions respond to whistle-blowers with the organizational equivalent of animal instinct," he told me. "They strike back. And the scope and intensity of their retaliation is directly related to the degree of threat that the whistle-blower is perceived to pose. The more significant a whistle-blower's disclosures, the greater the perceived need to take out the threat."

In that light, John Crane posed almost as big a threat as could be imagined, for his revelations called into question the very legitimacy of the whistle-blower protection system. After all, he had helped administer that system; he had championed its necessity; he had sought to protect it—and its clients, the whistle-blowers—from political interference. If he was now saying, under oath and penalty of perjury, that the system had been perverted, that its clients were being betrayed and punished rather than honored and protected, what did that say about the entire enterprise?

"It's a bit like a priest exposing the darkest secrets of the Catholic Church," I suggested, "your coming forward in this way. Isn't that what makes your case so threatening?"

"Absolutely," said Crane. "Maybe more like a bishop, though. I was high enough to see everything that was happening."

Crane rejected the idea that he was naïve about power. "I just want to see the system work properly," he said. "I know the system can fail—World War II, Nazi Germany—but I also know that you need to do what is right. Because the government is so powerful, you need to have it run efficiently and honestly and according to the law."

"What are the odds the system will work properly in your case?"

"I'm not giving you odds," he says with a chuckle. "This is just something that I have to do."

Perhaps the still-to-be-written conclusion of Crane's adventures would settle the matter. Would Secretary of

Defense Ashton Carter rule that his case should be heard? Would Crane get his job back? Would the case's resolution vindicate his faith in the justice of the system, or would it vindicate Devine's skepticism that whistle-blowers can get a fair shake?

All that was clear was that the conduct Crane witnessed inside the system had turned this whistle-blower protector into a whistle-blower himself. John Crane, The Third Man, had joined The Tribe.

The Future of the Tribe

E dward Snowden had more than one wish. Shortly after turning his life inside out by revealing some of the deepest secrets of the most powerful military empire in history, the former National Security Agency contract employee spoke with a reporter, Barton Gellman, of the *Washington Post* newspaper. Snowden's primary goal had been to alert people around the world to the extraordinary surveillance to which the United States government was subjecting them. He believed that Americans in particular had a right to know the broad outlines of the surveillance so they could decide whether the intrusion on personal privacy was worth the extra security it purportedly delivered.

But Snowden apparently had a second objective as well—to encourage more whistle-blowing. He "told me that he wanted to be actually a model for other whistle-blowers, that he wanted to show that you could come out and tell the truth about something you thought was wrong and you didn't have to hide," Gellman later told PBS's *Frontline*.

Hours after joining it, it seems, Edward Snowden was already trying to grow The Tribe.

Would Snowden get his wish? *Should* he?

"Given that Snowden has revealed how the US collects legitimate foreign intelligence and hurt our efforts against genuinely dangerous enemies like ISIS, I'm not sure that many will want to follow in his footsteps," Michael Hayden told me. In a March 2016 interview with television host Charlie Rose, Hayden added that "98 percent of what [Snowden] released has to do with how America collects foreign intelligence. What civil liberties quotient was there in giving a [media] correspondent a document that let him write about the ability of the NSA to intercept and penetrate the emails of the Syrian armed forces?"

If you've read this far in this book, you probably have opinions of your own about these questions. Because whether you love or hate him, detest or admire him, Edward Snowden and his whistle-blowing have transformed the world in which we all live. That gives each of us the right if not the responsibility to decide what we think about what he did and where it might lead next.

But if everyone is entitled to his or her own opinions, no one is entitled to their own facts. So let's review the evidence. Let's separate the documented facts about Snowden's whistle-blowing from the mountains of hearsay, politically charged accusations, and inaccurate information surrounding it. Let's summarize what Snowden actually did, and the results it provoked, so we can evaluate whether his example is or isn't likely to lead others to blow the whistle.

A Public Interest Defense—Prohibited

As of spring 2016, Snowden was still on the run from the US government. As far as the outside world knew, he was somewhere in Russia. He seemed to have easy access to Moscow, where on occasion he met visiting journalists and supporters.

Snowden was not in Russia because he wanted to be. Who would choose to give up the balmy breezes of Honolulu for the wintry gloom of Moscow? No, he got stranded there in June 2013 while trying to change planes on his way from Hong Kong, where he had given the secret NSA documents to journalists Laura Poitras, Glenn Greenwald, and Ewen MacAskill, to another location, apparently in South America. When the US government learned that Snowden was in the Moscow airport, it revoked his passport and demanded his extradition. The Russian government refused and eventually granted him asylum for one year, later extended to three years. Snowden had repeatedly denied accusations that, as a quid pro quo, he gave US secrets to Russia (or, while in Hong Kong, to China). He left all the documents with Poitras and Greenwald, he said, explaining that he had no interest in helping other governments. No evidence has surfaced to the contrary.

Unless Snowden had somehow slipped across the border, he was still in Russia. Journalists quoted him saying that his girlfriend, Lindsay Mills, had come to live with him (they are reportedly planning to marry), and he maintained a public presence, appearing at conferences and giving interviews via a de facto television studio he built inside his apartment. He went out occasionally but not often and claimed he didn't miss it. "I'm an indoor cat," he explained—content as long as he had a secure Internet connection whereby he could read, think, and communicate with the outside world.

It remained a puzzle why the US government, with its powerful surveillance capacity and many current and former officials yearning for Snowden's scalp, had not been able to locate Snowden. Or had it located him but chosen not to act, at least not yet? After all, what practical options did the United States have? Washington dared not try to kidnap or kill Snowden while he was in Russia; violating the territory of a country with its own vast national security complex was a price too high. But having Snowden roughed up on the street was certainly a plausible ploy, provided such an assault could not be traced back to the United States—which couldn't be a very pleasant thought for Snowden as he stepped out to do his grocery shopping.

Snowden has often said that he hopes to return to the United States someday. Indeed, he would come back tomorrow, if he thought he could get a fair trial. But that door seems closed. Indeed, Daniel Ellsberg told the young whistleblower during a visit to Moscow in summer 2015 that he might not ever see home again. "I do not think he will ever be able to come back to the United States no matter how popular he might come to be, and I think there is much more support for him month by month as people come to realize how little substance in the charges that he caused harm to us," Ellsberg told the *Guardian* in London on his way to see Snowden. "But that does not mean the intelligence community will ever forgive him for having exposed what they were doing. I don't think any president will find it politic to confront the intelligence community by pardoning him or allowing him to come back."

The official US position is clear and all but unanimous on the part of Republicans and Democrats alike: Snowden broke the law, he should come home, be put on trial, and sent to prison. To be sure, most officials didn't put it that bluntly;

Hillary Clinton said during the first Democratic presidential debate of the 2016 campaign that Snowden should "face the music."

What went unstated was that this music, legally speaking, was rigged against Snowden. And not just Snowden: any whistle-blower in the national security sphere faced the same daunting set of judicial rules.

At the core of those rules was the fact that US law prohibited national security whistle-blowers from mounting a "public interest defense." During a trial, Snowden could not utter so much as a syllable about his *reasons* for doing what he did. He could not explain that he had only leaked top-secret documents in order to alert the American people to violations of their Fourth Amendment rights. He could not argue that he broke one law—the law against disclosing classified information to unauthorized individuals—only to expose the breaking of *other* laws by senior government officials. He could not, in short, defend his actions by invoking their value to the "public interest."

The same legal restrictions confronted Ellsberg after he leaked the Pentagon Papers in 1971. The former US Marine Corps officer wanted to call witnesses at his trial who could testify to the deceptions of US officials about the Vietnam War and the resulting human costs. His lawyers, however, explained that a judge would immediately rule such efforts out of order. The only question before the court would be whether Ellsberg had in fact leaked classified information to unauthorized individuals. If so, the judge would have little or no leeway; the verdict would be guilty.

Although rarely mentioned in US media coverage, the prohibition against a public interest defense was arguably the most important legal fact confronting Snowden—and for that matter Thomas Drake, Jeffrey Sterling, and other national security whistle-blowers. The only question a court could consider in their cases would be whether these individuals had in fact leaked classified information: yes or no? But Snowden never denied having leaked such information. On the contrary, like Ellsberg before him, Snowden identified himself as the leaker in order to shield his workplace colleagues from suspicion.

The prohibition against a public interest defense was not without its justifications. If one accepted that a government must have the right to keep certain things secret, to forbid certain actions in the name of the common good, and to require its employees to carry out directives to deliver functioning governance, then a public interest defense could not be absolutely unfettered. Government workers could not decide which laws they obeyed and which they didn't. No government could carry out its functions and responsibilities under such circumstances. So where to draw the line?

"We need to strike a balance," argued Bea Edwards of GAP. "In the post-9/11 era the pendulum swung way too far towards security; the government is concealing things that just don't need to be concealed. Where the balance should be struck begins with that it should never be a crime to report a crime. If a government or corporation is harming the public and lying about it, a whistleblower should have freedom to report that to the public.

"What we advocate is a public interest defense," Edwards added. "If you're being persecuted, or prosecuted, because you spoke up for the public interest, a whistleblower should be able to defend what he or she did by proving, by some standard, that the exposé was in the public interest."

Michael Hayden took an opposing view. He criticized—but misrepresented—the public interest defense as meaning that "It doesn't really matter that I broke the law. I did a good thing, and I should only be judged on your appreciation of how good a thing I did." I guess that would be attractive to some people, but if you look at the American history of civil disobedience and you read Thoreau, it only becomes a morally justifiable act if you're prepared to pay the consequences.

Meanwhile, returning to the United States would be a dead end for Snowden. The prohibition against mounting a public interest defense would turn the legal proceedings against him into little more than a show trial and ensure his imprisonment. Why volunteer for that? "I expect to continue to live in exile for some time," he said in September 2015.

Nevertheless, the legal and emotional difficulties confronting Snowden, including his separation from family, friends, and homeland, were offset by the satisfaction of having accomplished his mission. "I can't live with my family nowadays," Snowden said via satellite to a gathering at New York's New School in February 2015. "I can't go back to my home. . . . But it's incredibly satisfying to be part of something larger than yourself. . . . And it has had a tremendous impact."

"All I wanted was for the public to have a say in how they are governed," he told Gellman in what the reporter said was the first interview Snowden gave from Russia, published in the *Washington Post* in December 2013. Gellman listed some of the extraordinary political, business, and judicial developments Snowden had triggered. The "basic structure of the Internet itself is now in question," Gellman wrote, "as Brazil and members of the European Union consider measures to keep their data away from US territory and US technological giants including Google, Microsoft and Yahoo take extraordinary steps to block the collection of data by their government." What's more, the NSA was under legal scrutiny like never before. Ruling on "a lawsuit that could not have gone forward without the disclosures made by Snowden," Richard

Leon, a US District Court judge, described the NSA's surveillance powers as "almost Orwellian" and said its bulk collection of US domestic telephone records was "probably unconstitutional."

The Supreme Court may eventually have to decide this issue, for days after Gellman's piece appeared, a second federal judge ruled that the surveillance program *was* constitutional. Echoing the arguments of Michael Hayden, District Judge William Pauley III argued that if the surveillance program had been in place before 9/11, "it would have furnished the missing information" needed to inform authorities that Khalid al-Mihdhar, the San Diego hijacker, was inside the United States.

Glenn Greenwald claimed an even longer list of accomplishments for Snowden. In his book, *No Place To Hide*, Greenwald argued that the disclosures he helped Snowden publicize have had effects "far greater, more enduring and more wide-ranging than we ever dreamed possible." Above all, they had "focused the world's attention on the dangers of ubiquitous state surveillance and pervasive government secrecy" and "triggered the first global debate about the value of individual privacy in the digital age." They "changed the way people around the world viewed the reliability of any statements made by US officials" and gave rise to "an ideologically diverse, trans-partisan coalition pushing for meaningful reform of the surveillance state."

What about the personal price Snowden paid? Greenwald exulted that Snowden "managed to remain free, outside the grasp of the United States," and he added that "There is a powerful lesson here for future whistle-blowers: speaking the truth does not have to destroy your life."

Snowden himself was less sanguine about this last item, perhaps because he had to live with the choices he made, not merely ponder them in the abstract. "Whistle-blowers," he said after two years of living in exile, "are elected by circumstance. Nobody self-nominates to be a whistle-blower, because it's so painful. Your lives are destroyed, regardless of whether you're right or wrong . . . . This is not something people sign up for."

Should Reporting a Crime Be a Crime?

Armed with this brief recapitulation of Snowden's experience, what do you think? Is his example likely to inspire others with inside information to step forward and blow the whistle?

Put differently, would Snowden's example inspire you? What if it were you who had inside information about deeply troubling institutional behavior? Knowing what this book has described about what happened to Snowden—and, if you've read the earlier chapters, what happened to Ellsberg, Drake and the NSA 4+1, Sterling, John Crane, and a host of other whistle-blowers from both the public and private sectors— would you choose to speak out and face the consequences?

Consider carefully. It's a decision that will change your life one way or the other forever.

If you do blow the whistle, you may bring about important, even life-saving, changes for yourself and your fellow citizens. But there is no guarantee of such a consequential outcome; in fact, the odds are against it. Meanwhile, you will almost certainly face harsh retaliation from the powers that be, risking your career, reputation, and financial and personal well-being. The only thing you can count on is "the satisfaction of knowing you did the right thing," to repeat what Tom Devine of the Government Accountability Project said earlier in this book.

On the other hand, if you don't speak out, you'll have to live with that as well. You'll have to live with the knowledge that you knew about something that was dangerous, illegal, or morally questionable, and you chose to remain silent to protect your own hide. That knowledge too imposes a burden, especially if other people end up suffering as a result.

Ray McGovern, the former CIA officer who witnessed the meeting between Snowden and Thomas Drake in Moscow, has lived with this knowledge for decades. As a young intelligence analyst during the Vietnam War, McGovern was friendly with another analyst, Sam Adams, who had authored a classified report revealing that the true number of enemy troops facing the United States in Vietnam was almost twice as high as the Pentagon was saying. Adams told McGovern that the Pentagon didn't want the higher number revealed for fear it would undermine the US government's efforts to portray the war as a success.

"I thought, *Somebody should get that memo and take it to the* New York Times," McGovern told me. "I could have asked Sam to give me a copy. But I didn't have the courage to do that. I had a mortgage, I had a new posting coming up in Germany, and all the other explanations would-be whistle-blowers have rolling around in their head were rolling around in my head. So what was the result? At the time [of Adams's memo], there were approximately 25,000 US forces killed and maybe a million Vietnamese. By the end of the war, each of those figures had more than doubled. What bothered Sam and me later was the thought that if we had gone public, the whole left side of the Vietnam memorial wouldn't be there. That's a heavy burden to carry around."

Such are the moral quandaries and calculations that confront any potential whistle-blower. And there is no one-size-fits-all answer for how to respond. Almost every whistle-blower I've known says that you don't really know how you will react until you find yourself in the actual situation.

Very few whistle-blowers go looking for trouble. Mostly, they are conscientious employees just doing their jobs until one day, they begin noticing things that don't seem right. Over time, the improprieties accumulate. They bring the problem to the attention of colleagues, of bosses, but for various reasons, the problem persists. Eventually, the moral quandary arises: one either remains silent about something that is wrong or dangerous, or one speaks out and faces the consequences.

"I imagine everyone's experience [on the way to becoming a whistle-blower] is different," Snowden said. "But for me, there was no single moment. It was seeing a continuing litany of lies from senior officials to Congress—and therefore to the American people—and the realization that Congress . . . wholly supported the lies, that compelled me to act."

Snowden has pronounced himself satisfied with his choice, despite its personal and emotional costs. After all, he accomplished much more than he expected when he first made the decision to speak out. Remember, at that point he feared that the public reaction would be a "collective shrug"—there would be no debate, much less reform, of the surveillance he was exposing. In which case he would have ruined his life for nothing. Obviously, it didn't work out that way.

But the key to understanding Snowden's whistle-blowing is the fact that he came forward despite his fear that little would come of it. Run the movie of his life backwards for a moment, back to the months and days before he leaked top-secret information to the press. At that point, there was no assurance whatsoever that his disclosures would accomplish anything beyond putting a target on his forehead.

Snowden spoke out anyway—not because he thought his odds of achieving something were good, but because he felt he had to try, no matter the odds.

It is this impulse that makes the Edward Snowdens and Daniel Ellsbergs and Thomas Drakes of the world whistle-blowers. To say that they choose not to remain silent isn't quite right; it's more accurate to say that they *cannot* choose to remain silent. They feel compelled to speak out, despite the risks and costs. Their consciences allow them no other course.

This quality—what I called "moral stubbornness" earlier in this book—simultaneously sets whistle-blowers apart from the rest of us and highlights the vital contribution they make to our collective well-being. Most people in their shoes would look the other way, keep their mouths shut, take the path of least resistance. Afterwards they might rationalize their inaction by assuring themselves that you can't fight City Hall. Not so with whistle-blowers. They come forward, when most of us won't, to identify problems that cry out for exposure. They are brave, yes, but more than that, they are self-sacrificing. They do what they do not for themselves but for the common good. And they usually end up paying a steep price.

For this, we owe whistle-blowers our respect and gratitude. We may or may not agree with the particular secrets a given whistle-blower exposes. But whatever our political leanings, whatever community or country we inhabit, we all benefit from the ecumenical willingness of members of the whistle-blower tribe to reveal things that otherwise would be kept hidden.

"With the 'watchdogs' in Congress now cheerleaders for the intelligence agencies rather than guardians of the public interest, and the [Foreign Intelligence Surveillance Court] neutered by the FISA Amendments Act, whistle-blowers are really the last best check on the government," said James Bamford, the author known for his decades of studying the NSA. "They're a courageous and precious resource."

As such, everyone has an interest in ensuring whistle-blowers the right to speak out when necessity compels. Which means, among other things, that whistle-blowers and whistle-blowing must be protected and encouraged. In particular, whistle-blowers need strong, well-enforced laws, responsible media coverage, and steadfast public support.

Alas, this is far from the situation today. Even in the United States, which on paper boasts the most extensive body of whistle-blower law in the world and relatively few official restrictions on press freedom, the whistle-blower proceeds at his or her peril, as the stories recounted in this book illustrate all too clearly.

Overseas the problem is, in general, worse. Most countries have no laws explicitly referencing whistle-blowing, leaving would-be truth-tellers judicially naked before the powers that be. The situation is especially challenging in countries ruled by authoritarian governments, where only the bravest of the brave speak out.

I had the honor some years ago of interviewing one such brave whistle-blower, a former Russian nuclear submarine commander named Alexander Nikitin. As I wrote in the *Los Angeles Times* in September 2000, "Nikitin's troubles with the authorities began in 1996, when he made world headlines by exposing what he called 'a Chernobyl in slow motion'—the Russian navy's reckless dumping of mothballed nuclear submarines in the Barents Sea and Kola Peninsula . . . . Nikitin included only previously published information in his exposé. Nevertheless, the Federal Security Service, Russia's recast KGB, charged him with espionage—on the basis of a law written months after he was imprisoned. Nikitin spent

151

10 months in jail and three years fighting his way through the court system." He was eventually acquitted by the City Court of St. Petersburg, but the federal authorities weren't done with him yet. In a maneuver of Kafkaesque absurdity, prosecutors swiftly sought a new trial. On what grounds? Why, because the government had violated Nikitin's rights the first time it tried to convict him.

Whistle-blower rights turn out to be an excellent barometer of democratic rights in general. Ensuring the right of individuals to challenge authority is, after all, an acid test of whether a government is accountable to the citizenry as a whole: are government officials above the law or subject to the same rules as everyone else?

This principle has been recognized by the European Union, at least in regards to countries of the former Soviet bloc. In the wake of the Soviet Union's collapse, many of those countries wanted to join the EU. One criterion the EU stipulated as part of the entry process was the establishment and strict enforcement of whistle-blower protection laws and regulations.

Who did the EU hire to help former Soviet-bloc countries write those laws? The Government Accountability Project, of course. Tom Devine made more than a dozen trips behind the former Iron Curtain to educate and assist legal teams in Slovakia, the Czech Republic, and Serbia as they drafted modern whistle-blower laws. "It's fulfilling work, to be there at the creation of a new legal system," said Devine. "Serbia, for example, now has the strongest whistle-blower law in the world," he added, "significantly stronger than in the United States."

One central principle of Serbia's new whistle-blower laws would have a direct bearing on Snowden's case. The principle: it is not a crime to report a crime. If a whistle-blower provides evidence that, say, a government official or government agency has engaged in criminal activity, the whistle-blower cannot be prosecuted simply because other laws forbid the disclosure of such activity. This principle in effect opens the door to the "public interest defense" that US law prohibits. If this principle were applied in the United States, a legal proceeding against Snowden could no longer be restricted to the narrow question of whether he had revealed classified information or not. "I'd be thrilled if we could have Serbia's new whistle-blower law here in the US," said Devine.

Meanwhile, public education and mobilization are vital, said Norman Solomon, whose work on behalf of Jeffrey Sterling led to the founding of the nonprofit project ExposeFacts.org. "If people don't realize how much they owe to whistle-blowers in their own lives, they can overlook how important whistle-blowers are," Solomon told me. "We want to bring whistle-blowing out of the shadows. It shouldn't be something that is furtive. We should bring it into the light, encourage and support it financially and through public education and activism.

"Reforming the role of journalism is critical," Solomon continued, arguing that, "Whistle-blowers shatter the stenography to power that corporate media often convey. For example, whistle-blowers remind us that governments lie, especially in times of war, whereas Americans usually get quite a different message from the corporate media."

Really? Americans don't know that their government lies?

"As an abstraction, many Americans know the government lies," Solomon replied. "But people forget it in the heat of the moment, as we saw when the Bush administration invaded Iraq on the basis of false claims about weapons of mass destruction—claims the corporate media, starting with the *New York Times*, were happy to amplify for months before the invasion. It's like history starts again and again."

Too much of the mainstream media, especially in Washington, is too close to the government, argued Jesselyn Radack, who left GAP to join ExposeFacts.org. Reflecting on her role as an attorney for Snowden, Drake, and other whistle-blowers, Radack told me that the Washington press corps' tendency to echo rather than question government officials meant that "the US government has the biggest megaphone in the world. If they want there to be a smear piece on Snowden, all they have to do is make a phone call and their story is on the front page of the *New York Times* or some other major outlet. Look at the headlines that ran after Snowden was stranded in the Moscow airport: 'Snowden Flees to Russia.' Not a single mainstream journalist called me, his attorney, to ask if that was true. If they had, I would have explained that he only ended up there because the US government cancelled his passport. Nobody bothered to ask."

Excessive closeness to the government not only complicates the news media's First Amendment role as a watchdog on government, it also can deter whistle-blowers from providing the kind of eye-catching exposés that attract audiences. Remember, this is what cost the *New York Times* the Snowden scoop. As Snowden told a *Times* reporter after the fact, the clincher was the newspaper's withholding, at the behest of the Bush administration, the publication of James Risen's and Eric Lichtblau's article. Snowden would not trust his story, and his life, to the *Times*, despite its reach and influence. The *Times*' loss was the *Guardian*'s gain—a lesson for journalists and their executive superiors everywhere.

Where Were the Exxon Whistle-blowers?

As I finished writing this book, a blockbuster news development offered valuable lessons about whistle-blowing. Two journalistic investigations published in fall 2015 revealed that Exxon had been lying for decades about global warming. According to exposés compiled separately by the *Los Angeles Times* and *Inside Climate News*, Exxon's top executives and its board of directors knew perfectly well by the mid-1980s that burning oil, gas, and other fossil fuels would raise global temperatures and unleash impacts—harsher heat waves, deeper droughts, stronger storms, faster sea level rise—that could imperil humanity's future. The oil giant's leaders knew these things because Exxon's own scientists had researched the issue extensively and reported their findings repeatedly. And management took the findings seriously; it even adjusted corporate practices. For example, when constructing new transportation facilities, Exxon engineers took the anticipated future sea level rise into account.

Subsequent reporting by *Inside Climate News* revealed that Exxon was not alone: Other oil companies were also aware of climate science in the 1980s—and likewise took steps to protect their own investments from the consequences.

But that was in private. Publicly, Exxon and its oil industry peers denied what they knew about climate change. Company executives and spokesmen insisted that the science behind man-made climate change was highly uncertain and therefore should not guide government policy. Exxon (later, ExxonMobil) led the charge. Beginning in 1997, the oil company spent at least $29.9 million to fund public relations groups, lobbying campaigns, and other efforts to portray man-made climate change as a "premise that . . . defies common sense" as Lee Raymond, ExxonMobil's chairman and CEO, argued in a 1997 speech opposing the Kyoto Protocol, an international treaty aimed at limiting greenhouse gas emissions.

Big Oil's lies had enormous effect. Combined with the political muscle that came from being the richest business enterprise in history, the misinformation Exxon and its corporate brethren peddled over the past three decades was the single most powerful obstacle to vigorous government action against climate change. Big Oil's influence was most apparent within the Republican Party, where rejection of mainstream climate science became a litmus test that virtually all GOP members of Congress and presidential candidates saluted. If not for this reflexive opposition, the US government would undoubtedly have taken stronger steps, sooner, to limit the fossil fuel burning that drives global warming.

The chain of causality extended still further, for action by the United States would have broken the stalemate that blocked international climate action for the past twenty-five years. During these years China and other emerging economies repeatedly asked, why should we cut our emissions when the biggest climate polluter on earth, the United States, refuses even to acknowledge the problem?

As I reported from the UN Paris climate summit in December 2015, the agreement reached there would have been much more ambitious if the US delegation did not have to worry that mandatory emissions cuts and other nonvoluntary measures would qualify the accord as a treaty and thus ensure its rejection by the Republican-dominated US Senate. Likewise, the summit's laudable goal—to limit temperature rise to "well below" 2 degrees Celsius above pre-industrial levels, and "to pursue" a limit of 1.5 C—would be much easier to attain post-Paris if fossil fuel interests and the politicians they buy had not blocked progress for the preceding two decades. Those two decades of emissions had helped to increase the global temperature to 1 degree C above the pre-industrial level, meaning that emissions post-Paris had to fall at a stunning pace.

"Crimes against humanity." That's what Hans Schellnhuber, the German scientist who advised Pope Francis on his 2015 climate change encyclical, *Laudato Si*, called the actions of climate science deniers and others who deliberately blocked corrective policies. By helping to keep carbon emissions rising for decades beyond when the company's own scientists knew that this invited disaster, Exxon's leaders helped to destabilize the climate that every person on earth relies upon for food, water, and other essentials of life. If that isn't a crime, what is?

As the father of an eleven-year-old daughter, I share Schellnhuber's view, and his anger. I know other parents who feel the same. Civil society—parents, climate activists, faith organizations, local and state governments, educational institutions, businesses and other commercial enterprises, and ordinary people throughout the world—are now called upon to push national governments to honor the Paris Agreement. The Paris outcome is one of numerous recent bright spots suggesting it is still possible to secure a livable planet for our children. Nevertheless, it remains a crime that we were put in this situation in the first place so that special interests could maximize their already bountiful profits.

Here's the whistle-blower connection: these crimes on the part of Exxon and other oil companies might have been halted if the outside world had learned about them sooner. If a whistle-blower from within Exxon—say, one of the scientists who did the research documenting that man-made global warming was real—had come forward to reveal these truths back in the 1980s, Exxon and the rest of Big Oil might not have gotten away with their treachery. If an Exxon insider had spoken out, the way tobacco industry scientist Jeffrey Wigand spoke out, things might have been different. The US media would have been less likely to fall for the lie that climate science was uncertain. Smarter news coverage would have kindled greater public awareness and calls for action. Government officials would have been more likely to treat climate change as the emergency it was, rather than to dodge, weave, deny, and delay. The world would be a safer place today.

Like Ray McGovern's guilty feelings about the names of tens of thousands of dead American troops on the left side of the Vietnam War Memorial, are there now former Exxon employees who regret not coming forward to expose their industry's lies? If there are, they haven't shared those feelings publicly. But they must live with their choice, and with our collective knowledge of it.

So anyone who thinks that whistle-blowing is a fool's errand or a fringe concern, please think again. That is not the lesson of the Exxon episode, or of the travails of Edward Snowden, Thomas Drake, John Crane, and the many other whistle-blowers featured in this book.

The truth, it seems to me, is that our lives, our liberty, and much else may depend on whistle-blowing and the tribe of singularly brave, eccentric, morally stubborn individuals who give it life. Whistle-blowers sometimes break the law. They are not always easy to deal with, and they are not always right. But without them, society—which is to say, all of us—risks tumbling into one disaster after another. Bless them, I say. Bless them, warts and all.

Endnotes

Most of the direct quotations contained in this book come from interviews the author conducted with the sources named. Only when this is not the case—for example, when a quotation was first reported by a news article—is a reference cited in these Notes. The same rule applies to general statements of fact, with an additional qualifier: if such statements derive from the author's interviews, or if the source of a statement is made clear in the narrative, no citation is give; if the statement derives from another source, that source is listed below.

Pg. 3: "It's fair to say . . .": AJ+, August 5, 2015: https://www.youtube.com/watch?v=MKnnnufSYLo/

Pg. 5: "political romantic . . .": *New York Times*, June 8, 2014: http://www.nytimes.com/2014/06/08/books/review/no-place-to-hide-by-glenn-greenwald.html

Pg. 7: "I only have one fear . . .": *No Place to Hide: Edward Snowden, the NSA, and U.S. Surveillance State, by Glenn Greenwald*, (New York: Picador, 2014), page 19

Pg. 9: "If you seek to help . . .": *Ibid*, page 32

Pg. 11: "a coward [who] betrayed his country...": NBC News, May 28, 2014: http://www.nbcnews.com/politics/first-read/kerry-snowden-coward-traitor-n116366

Pg. 12: "I must admit, in my darker moments . . .": *The Hill*, October 3, 2013: http://thehill.com/policy/technology/326315-former-nsa-chief-jokes-about-putting-snowden-on-kill-list

Pg. 12: James Woolsey's made his death sentence comments on CNN, November 19, 2015: http://www.cnn.com/videos/us/2015/11/19/ex-cia-director-james-woolsey-edward-snowden-intvw-nr.cnn

Pg. 12: "I would love to put a bullet . . .": *BuzzFeed,* January 16, 2014: http://www.buzzfeed.com/bennyjohnson/americas-spies-want-edward-snowden-dead#.rtMV5Q449Y

Pg. 12: "Snowden?' they asked . . .": *The Nation,* October 10, 2014: http://www.thenation.com/article/edward-snowden-speaks-sneak-peek-exclusive-interview/

Pg. 13: Kerry, Ellsberg comments about Snowden: *Huffington Post,* May 29, 2014: http://www.huffingtonpost.com/2014/05/29/daniel-ellsberg-john-kerry-snowden_n_5412980.html

Pg. 18: "I mean, who would believe . . .": New York Times, August 13, 2013: http://www.nytimes.com/2013/08/13/us/nsa-leaks-make-plan-for-cyberdefense-unlikely.html

Pg. 19: "The real issue is not just privacy . . .": Comments at the new School in New York City and recorded on video for "Times Talks": http://timestalks.com/laura-poitras-glenn-greenwald-edward-snowden.html

Pg. 25: Coleen Rowley's corrective letter: *The Guardian,* May 25, 2002: http://www.theguardian.com/world/2002/may/25/afghanistan.usa

Pg. 29: Hayden's Senate testimony is reference in *The Shadow Factory: The NSA from 9/11 to the Eavesdropping on America,* by James Bamford, (New York: Anchor, 2009), pg. 122

Pg. 32: "I'm sorry about that . . .": Poitras's documentary The Program: http://www.nytimes.com/video/opinion/100000001733041/the-program.html

Pg. 35: "Baginski reportedly told him . . .": "The Secret Sharer," by Jane Mayer, *The New Yorker,* May 23, 2011: http://www.newyorker.com/magazine/2011/05/23/the-secret-sharer

Pg. 38: "The case of Thomas Drake represented . . .": AJ+, August 5, 2015: https://www.youtube.com/watch?v=MKnnnufSYLo/

Pg. 41: Bradley Manning's leak to Wikileaks was detailed in "The Trials of Bradley Manning," by Janet Reitman, *Rolling Stone,* March 14, 2013: http://www.rollingstone.com/politics/news/the-trials-of-bradley-manning-20130314

Pg. 42: "I want people to see . . ." *Ibid.*

Pg. 49: Katharine Gun's whistle-blowing was described in *The Guardian*, January 31, 2016: http://www.theguardian.com/film/2016/jan/31/katharine-gun-observer-iraq-war-whistleblower-hollywood-film-official-secrets

Pg. 50: "The point is not . . .": The Washington Post, March 7, 1979: https://www.washingtonpost.com/archive/politics/1979/03/07/tapes-show-nixon-role-in-firing-of-ernest-fitzgerald/048cd88e-60e5-498d-a8e2-e3b39461356b/

Pg. 51: Charles Grassley comments about Earnest Fitzgerald on *Capitol Words*: http://capitolwords.org/date/2006/03/06/S1780-2_honoring-a-ernest-fitzgerald/

Pg. 52: "Other notable case" paragraph's whistleblower stories were told in *The Corporate Whistleblower's Survival Guide*, by Tom Devine and Tarek F. Maassarani (San Francisco: Berett-Koehler, 2011), pg. 13

Pg. 52: "For those who think": *Ibid*, pg. 18

Pg. 62: Ralph Nader's coining of the term "whistleblower" was reported in the Wall Street Journal, July 12, 2013: http://www.wsj.com/articles/SB1 0001424127887323368704578596083294221030

Pg. 63: GAP's strategies for "turning information into power" were described in *The Corporate Whistleblower's Survival Guide*, by Tom Devine and Tarek F. Maassarani (San Francisco: Berett-Koehler, 2011), *op. cit.*, pgs. 5 and 15

Pg. 69: The account of the Zimmer nuclear power plant is based on the author's interviews with Devine and Clark for *The New York Times*, January 22, 1984: http://www.nytimes.com/1984/01/22/us/nearly-completed-nuclear-plant-will-be-converted-to-burn-coal.html

Pg. 75: The story of Dr. Carl Teleen was told in *Blowing the Whistle: Dissent in the Public Interest*, by Charles Peters and Taylor Branch (New York: Praeger, 1972), pg. 244-245

Pg. 84: *The New York Times* published its Editor's Note about its inaccurate coverage of the build up to the Iraq war May 26, 2004: http://www.nytimes.com/2004/05/26/world/from-the-editors-the-times-and-iraq.html?_r=0

Pg. 85: My scoop was published in *Vanity Fair*, November 2003, "Nuclear Insecurity": http://www.vanityfair.com/news/2003/11/whistle-blowers-on-vulnerable-us-nuclear-facilities

Pg. 86: "I have values . . .": *The Whistleblower's Survival Guide: Courage Without Martyrdom*, Tom Devine (Washington, D.C.: The Fund for constitutional government, 1997), pg. 23

Pg. 94: Snowden's and Ellsberg's comments the Hope X conference: https://www.youtube.com/watch?v=YPdOOoNmYSQ

Pg. 100: Gustav von Rudel's affidavit providing a minute-by-minute eyewitness account of the Beer Hall Putsch—eight typewritten, single spaced pages in German—was submitted to the *Munchner Merkur* newspaper of Munich but inexplicably never published. Crane shared a copy of the affidavit, and an accompanying telegram from von Rudel affirming its authenticity, with the author, who can share it with anyone wishing to verify my greatly abbreviated summary of its contents. The affidavit and telegram are also published in full in an Appendix to the German edition of *Bravehearts*, issued by Hanser Verlag of Munich.

Pg. 104: "Under the current system . . .": http://www.grassley.senate.gov/news/news-releases/grassley-talks-about-anniversary-whistleblower-protection-act

Pg. 108; Congress's transfer of NSA's spending authority was reported by *The Baltimore Sun*, July 20, 2003: http://articles.baltimoresun.com/2003-07-20/news/0307200276_1_nsa-eavesdropping-agency/2; Congress's halting of the Traiblazer program was reported by Jane Mayer in *The New Yorker, op. cit.*

Pg. 109: Background on Dan Meyer and the USS Iowa tragedy: https://en.wikipedia.org/wiki/Daniel_P._Meyer

https://en.wikipedia.org/wiki/USS_Iowa_turret_explosion

Pg. 117: "We are now becoming a police state . . .": "The United States of Secrets," *Frontline*, May 13, 2014: http://www.pbs.org/wgbh/frontline/film/united-states-of-secrets/

Pg. 121: "[President Obama] could end mass surveillance . . .": *Times Talks, op cit.*

Pg. 122: "Baldly lying to the public": *The Snowden Files: The Inside Story of the World's Most Wanted Man*, by Luke Harding (New York: Vintage, 2014), page 52

Pg. 124: The FBI agents' views about Petraeus were reported in *The Washington Post*, April 23, 2014: https://www.washingtonpost.com/world/national-security/petraeus-set-to-plead-guilty-to-mishandling-

classified-materials/2015/04/22/3e6dbf20-e8f5-11e4-aae1-d642717d8
afa_story.html

Petraeus's speaking fees were reported in *The Daily Beast*, April 22, 2014:
http://www.thedailybeast.com/articles/2015/04/22/the-double-standard-
for-david-petraeus.html

Pg. 125: The description of Jeffrey Sterling's case is based on the
authors' interview with Norman Solomon and on Sterling's direct statements in the documentary *The Invisible Man*: https://exposefacts.org/
watch-the-short-documentary-the-invisible-man-nsa-whistleblow-
er-jeffrey-sterling/

Pg. 127: Holly Sterling's comments were reported on *Democracy Now!*,
October 15, 2015: http://www.democracynow.org/2015/10/15/breaking_
silence_wife_of_jailed_cia

Pg. 138: Hayden's interview with Charlie Rose broadcast on February 22,
2016: http://www.charlierose.com/watch/60690778

Pg. 139: "I'm an indoor cat,": *The Nation*, October 10, 2014: , *op. cit.*

Pg. 140: Snowden expressed his desire to return to the US if he could
get a fair trial during an interview on *Al Jazeera America*, September 4,
2015: http://www.aljazeera.com/programmes/upfront/2015/09/edward-
snowden-speaks-mehdi-hasan-150904102133681.html

Pg. 140: "I do not think he will ever be able to come back . . .": *The
Guardian*, June 1, 2015: http://www.theguardian.com/us-news/2015/
jun/01/edward-snowden-nsa-surveillance-patriot-act-whistleblow-
ers-daniel-ellsberg

Pg. 142: Hayden criticized the public interest defense on the Charlie Rose
Show, *op. cit.*

Pg. 142: "I expect to continue to live in exile . . ." *Al Jazeera America, op. cit.*

Pg. 143: "I can't live with my family . . .": *Times Talks, op. cit.*

Pg. 143: "All I wanted was . . .": Washington Post, December 23,
2014: https://www.washingtonpost.com/world/national-security/
edward-snowden-after-months-of-nsa-revelations-says-his-missions-
accomplished/2013/12/23/49fc36de-6c1c-11e3-a523-fe73f0ff6b8d_
story.html

Pg. 143: Judge Pauley's ruling was reported in *The Huffington Post*,
December 27, 2013: http://www.huffingtonpost.com/2013/12/27/nsa-lawsuit-
dismissed_n_4508903.html

Pg. 144: Greenwald's list of Snowden's accomplishments is found in *No Place to Hide, op. cit.* pgs. 248-249 and 253

Pg. 144: "Whistleblowers are elected by circumstance . . .": comments to KALW public radio program, *Philosophy Talk*, July 12, 2015: http://kalw.org/post/philosophy-talk-asks-edward-snowden-about-ethics-whistleblowing#stream/0

Pg. 149: I reported on Nikitin in *The Los Angeles Times* on September 11, 2000: http://articles.latimes.com/2000/sep/11/local/me-19219

Pg. 152: The initial *Inside Climate News* investigations of Exxon began to be published on September 16, 2015: http://insideclimatenews.org/news/15092015/Exxons-own-research-confirmed-fossil-fuels-role-in-global-warming

The first *Los Angeles Times* investigation (in collaboration with the Columbia University School of Journalism) was published October 9, 2015: http://graphics.latimes.com/exxon-arctic/

Pg. 153: The Inside Climate News investigation of Exxon's oil industry peers was published on December 22, 2015: http://insideclimatenews.org/news/22122015/exxon-mobil-oil-industry-peers-knew-about-climate-change-dangers-1970s-american-petroleum-institute-api-shell-chevron-texaco

Pg. 153: Exxon's $29.9 million spent on climate disinformation efforts was reported by "Exxon Secrets," a research unit at Greenpeace USA: http://www.exxonsecrets.org/html/index.php

Pg. 153: Lee Raymond's premise that . . . defies common sense" quote was reported in *Private Empire: ExxonMobil and American Power* by Steve Coll (New York: Penguin, 2012), pgs. 81-83, 190, and 534-537

Pg. 154: I discussed how climate-denying Republicans weakened the Paris Agreement in The Nation, December 14, 2015: http://www.thenation.com/article/the-fate-of-the-world-changed-in-paris-but-by-how-much/

Pg. 154: I first reported Hans Schellnhuber's "crimes against humanity in my book, *Hot: Living through the Next Fifty Years on Earth* (Boston: Houghton Mifflin Harcourt, 2011), pg. 254-255